HISTORY OF ENGLISH VERSIONS OF THE BIBLE

FREDERIC G. KENYON &
EDWARD D. ANDREWS

"I believe that the time has come ... to restore confidence in the Bible as a guide to truth and a basis for the conduct of life."
—Sir Frederic G. Kenyon

HISTORY OF ENGLISH VERSIONS OF THE BIBLE

"I believe that the time has come ... to restore confidence in the Bible as a guide to truth and a basis for the conduct of life."
—Sir Frederic G. Kenyon

The Truth Shall Set You Free

Frederic G. Kenyon &
Edward D. Andrews

Christian Publishing House

Cambridge, Ohio

CHRISTIAN PUBLISHING HOUSE

CONSERVATIVE CHRISTIAN BOOKS

APOLOGETIC DEFENSE OF GOD, THE
FAITH, THE BIBLE, AND CHRISTIANITY

Unless otherwise stated, Scripture quotations are from the Updated American Standard Version (UASV) Copyright © 2018 by Christian Publishing House

HISTORY OF ENGLISH VERSIONS OF THE BIBLE

Authored by Frederic G. Kenyon & Edward D Andrews

ISBN-13: **978-1-949586-97-8**

ISBN-10: **1-949586-97-9**

TRANSLATIONS Referred to in this Publication

Unless otherwise indicated, Scripture quotations are from the *Updated American Standard Version of the Holy Scriptures,* 2016 (UASV). Abbreviations used to designate other translations of the Bible are provided below:

ASV: American Standard Version (1901)

AMP: Amplified Bible (1987)

AT: The Bible – An American Translation (1935)

CEB: Common English Bible (2011)

CEV: Contemporary English Version (1995)

DARBY: Darby Translation (1890)

ERV: Easy to Read Version (2012)

GW: GOD'S WORD Translation (1995)

GNT: Good News Translation (1992)

HCSB: Holman Christian Standard Bible (2003)

JB: The Jerusalem Bible (1966)

JP: The Holy Scriptures According to the Masoretic Text (1917)

KJV: King James Version (1611, 1942)

LEB: Lexham English Bible (LEB)

LXX: Greek Septuagint Version of Hebrew Old Testament (280-150 B.C.E.)

NCV: New Century Version (2005)

NEB: New English Bible (1970)

NLV: New Life Version (1969)

NLT: New Living Translation (2013)

NTB: A New Translation of the Bible (1934)

NASB: New American Standard Bible (1995)

NET: New English Translation (2006) Biblical Studies Press

NIV: New International Version (2011)

NIVI: New International Version Inclusive Language Edition (1996)

NKJV: New King James Version (1982)

NLT: New Living Translation (2007)

NLV: New Language Version (1969)

NRSV: New Revised Standard Version (1989)

PHILIPS: New Testament in Modern English (1958)

REB: Revised English Bible (1989)

RSV: Revised Standard Version (1971)

SEB: Simple English Bible (1980)

TEB: The Emphasised Bible (1897)

TEV: Today's English Version (1976)

TLB: The Living Bible (1971)

TNIV: Today's New International Version (2005)

UASV: Updated American Standard Version (2013-18 Work in progress)[1]

WHNU: Westcott-Hort Greek New Testament / Nestle-Aland Greek New Testament, United Bible Society Greek New Testament (1881, 2012, 1993)

YLT: Young's Literal Translation (1887)

---

[1] The UASV is projected to be completed by 2019. However, we are using verses herein of the books that are completed at present.

INTRODUCTION Bible Translation Is a Hazardous Duty

Edward D. Andrews

Bible translation goes back to 280 to 150 B.C.E., when (seventy-two, according to tradition) translators gave us the Hebrew Old Testament books in Greek. From those days forward, translators have lived very dangerous lives, in trying to bring us the Word of God in the common languages of man. Most times this has been from the religious organizations themselves, who have caused the suffering and death of many translators.

The English Bible

The English Bible translation came to us in the late fourteenth century. John Wycliffe (c. 1328 – December 31, 1384), is the one credited with the handwritten translation. However, it was not rendered from the original language texts of Hebrew and Greek, but from the Latin Vulgate. Therefore, it was a translation of a translation. Exactly how much of the translation

Wycliffe completed before his death in 1384 is unknown. However, what we do know is that there was strong opposition to his work. Both Wycliffe and those helping received bitter hatred from the religious leaders of his day. If it were not for his influence, he would have been martyred like many others.

However, the story of Wycliffe does not end with his death. The Church leadership continued to oppose the copying of the Wycliffe translation. Some 24-years after Wycliffe's death, in 1408, a Church council met in Oxford at the direction of Archbishop Arundel, prohibiting the use of the Holy Scriptures in English. This ban by the clergy was not going to stand up as the people wanted to have a copy of the only English translation available to them. We have evidence of such, as we possess today nearly 200 copies of the Wycliffe translation, many that were made after 1420. John Wycliffe was so despised that these religious leaders had his bones dug up in 1428 to be burned, with the ashes to be cast into the river Swift.

William Tyndale

It would not be until the sixteenth century that we would see a translation that was rendered from the original language texts of Hebrew and Greek. It would be the William Tyndale, who would bring us our first printed English translation. Thinking that he could acquire the backing of Bishop Cuthbert Tunstall, Tyndale went to London. However, he was unsuccessful in getting the bishop's support.

While still in London, Tyndale came to the realization that there would be no translation with the current attitude of the religious leaders in England. Therefore, in 1524 he headed for Germany. Once in Cologne, the translation of the New Testament got under way. However, the magistrates of Cologne were none too happy about this news as it reached them. Thus, they put a stop to the work. This forced Tyndale to move on to Worms;

there the printing of the New Testament was finally completed. In time, translations of this New Testament were flooding England. Meanwhile, back in Worms, Tyndale continued his revision work on the translation.

Needless to say, the English church authorities were beside themselves with rage. On May 4, 1530, copies of Tyndale's translation were burned at St. Paul's Cross in London. At the end of May, there was a royal decree backed by the church authorities, which listed the translation of Tyndale among wicked books and stated, "Detest them, abhor them; keep them not in your hands, deliver them to the superiors such as call for them." For those that would think of ignoring the decree, it continued, "The prelates of the church, having the care and charge of your souls, ought to compel you, and your prince to punish and correct you." There was no effort spared in attempts at destroying the translations in England.

One of the reasons for such great hatred on the part of the religious leaders was Tyndale's choice renderings of some terms. For instance, he chose to use "congregation" over "church;" "overseer" instead of "bishop;" and "love" in place of "charity." It did not matter to the religious authorities that his choice of words was more accurate as to the original language terms. Even still, Tyndale had said he would correct anything that was proven inaccurate, or that could be translated more clearly. The fact of the matter was that the religious authorities knew that these renderings affected the power of the church, giving the power back to the people.

In time, Tyndale's efforts were to come to a close, as a man named Phillips pretended to be his friend and then betrayed him like Judas had done Christ. Tyndale was arrested and imprisoned in the castle of Vilvorde, near Brussels. In September of 1536, he was executed by being strangling and burned.

The man, William Tyndale, a great scholar, set the foundation of translation from the 1611 King James Version, which was 90 percent Tyndale up unto the 2001 English Standard Version. Tyndale knowing that day-in-and-day-out, his life was at risk, but he sought to bring to the English world, the Word of God, and not for glory or honor, but for the love of God and neighbor. There are dozens of men and women, who have suffered martyrdom to bring us God's Word. Truly, the Bible translator has taken on a very dangerous task.

1 Timothy 2:3-4 Updated American Standard Version (UASV)

³ his is good, and it is acceptable in the sight of God our Savior, ⁴ who desires all men to be saved and to come to an accurate knowledge[2] of truth.

The Life and Martyrdom John Hus (1369-1415)

In the first century of our common era, the first martyr gave his life because of his stance for God, Stephen. (Acts 7:54-6) These early disciples of Christ had been given a commission that all Christians are expected to carry out:

Matthew 24:14: "this gospel of the kingdom will be proclaimed throughout the whole world."

Matthew 28:19-20: "Go therefore and make disciples of all nations ... teaching them to observe all that I have commanded you."

Acts 1:8: "you will be my witnesses in Jerusalem and in all Judea and Samaria, and to the end of the earth."

Stephen is seized, gives fearless witness, and dies a martyr for daring to bear witness about Christ. James died about 44 C.E. Herod Agrippa I had him executed with the sword. He was the first of the 12 Apostles to die as a martyr. (Ac 12:1-3) The rest of the book of Acts encompasses an unforgettable record of the judgments, imprisonment, and maltreatment, harassment, and downright oppression endured by faithful ones like Peter, and the Apostle Paul, the former persecutor turned apostle, who suffered martyrdom at the hands of Roman Emperor Nero about 65 C.E. – 2 Corinthians 11:23-27; 2 Timothy 4:6-8.

---

[2] *Epignosis* is a strengthened or intensified form of *gnosis* (*epi*, meaning "additional"), meaning, "true," "real," "full," "complete" or "accurate," depending upon the context. Paul and Peter alone use *epignosis*.

The Apostles Arrested and Freed

Acts 5:17-18 English Standard Version (ESV)

[17] But the high priest rose up, and all who were with him (that is, the party of the Sadducees), and filled with jealousy [18] they arrested the apostles and put them in the public prison.

The Angel of the Lord

Acts 5:19-21 English Standard Version (ESV)

[19] But during the night an angel of the Lord opened the prison doors and brought them out, and said, [20] "Go and stand in the temple and speak to the people all the words of this Life." [21] And when they heard this, they entered the temple at daybreak and began to teach. Now when the high priest came, and those who were with him, they called together the council, all the senate of the people of Israel, and sent to the prison to have them brought.

The Astonishment of the Jailers

Acts 5:22-26 English Standard Version (ESV)

[22] But when the officers came, they did not find them in the prison, so they returned and reported, [23] "We found the prison securely locked and the guards standing at the doors, but when we opened them we found no one inside." [24] Now when the captain of the temple and the chief priests heard these words, they were greatly perplexed about them, wondering what this would come to. [25] And someone came and told them, "Look! The men whom you put in prison are standing in the temple and teaching the people." [26] Then the captain with the officers went and brought them, but not by force, for they were afraid of being stoned by the people.

The Accusation by the Sanhedrin

Acts 5:27-28 English Standard Version (ESV)

[27] And when they had brought them, they set them before the council. And the high priest questioned them, [28] saying, "We strictly charged you not to teach in this name, yet here you have filled Jerusalem with your teaching, and you intend to bring this man's blood upon us."

The Answer by the Apostles

Acts 5:29-32 English Standard Version (ESV)

[29] But Peter and the apostles answered, "<u>We must obey God rather than men</u>. [30] The God of our fathers raised Jesus, whom you killed by hanging him on a tree. [31] God exalted him at his right hand as Leader and Savior, to give repentance to Israel and forgiveness of sins. [32] And we are witnesses to these things, and so is the Holy Spirit, whom God has given to those who obey him."

Ever since that unforgettable first-century, many have boldly followed in the footsteps of Jesus and those first martyrs. Those first-century Christian martyrs stood their ground against the religious leaders of their day, who did not want to hear the truth, and would execute anyone try to share the good news of the kingdom. (Matthew 23:13) This appendix is featuring just such a person, one who stood in the face of a very powerful religious system and refused to back down. John Hus (1371-1415) used those very same words of the Apostle Peter when he was ordered not to preach in his fellow Bohemians. He accepted the supreme authority of God and His Word at a time when virtually everyone else viewed the pope and the church as supreme. How did he come to take this stand?

The Early Life and Bible Teachings of John Hus

The mother of John Hus was a widow and a peasant, which means that the family would have struggled for the simple necessities of like, let alone an education. Like Martin Luther, he chose to sing and perform services in churches to earn a living for the family. Initially, his desire to consider being of the clergy was because of their lifestyle that was free from the stresses of the day. As a student at the University of Prague Hus did not distinguish himself, as he was not a brilliant young man by any means. In 1393, he received his Bachelor of Arts, in 1394 Bachelor of Theology, and in 1396 Master of Arts. In around 1400, he was able to become an ordained priest; in 1401, he became dean of the philosophical faculty, and in the following year rector of the university. In addition, in 1402, he was chosen to preach at the Bethlehem Church in Prague, where he preached in the Czech language.

Throughout this period, there was much conflict between the Germans and the Czechs in the university. Hus would become a defender of the Czech cause, all the while his influence was growing because his preaching was becoming all the more powerful. Since 1382, the writings of the English Morning Star of Reformers, John Wycliffe had been pouring into Bohemia, and Hus had been taking them in all through his student days, especially the work On Truth of Holy Scripture, which he obtained in 1407. All the while, there had been a discontent and debate over many mistreatments involving the Roman Catholic Church. While many believe that the Bohemian Reformation only came about because of the stirrings in England, this just is not the case; they ran parallel to each other.

One line of opposition came from Archbishop Zbynek of Prague, who took exception to Hus' preaching. To get even with Hus, Zbynek publicly burned the writings of Wycliffe in 1410. Another tactic to shut Hus out was to forbid preaching except in recognized churches, which would exclude the Bethlehem Chapel where Hus presided. Well, like any good reformer, Hus chose to disobey the archbishop's prohibition, stating that he had to "obey God rather than men in things which are necessary for salvation." Hus chose rather to take his case to the pope but was excommunicated by the archbishop for his efforts. However, Hus did not falter, finding that his better understanding had honed his conscience and made it more sensitive to the Word of God. He clearly stated, "Man may lie, but God lies not," stressing the Apostle Paul's words to the Romans. (Romans 3:4) King Wenceslas defended Hus' reform movement, and eventually, Zbynek took flight out of the country, dying shortly thereafter.

Hostility and opposition were soon Hus' bedfellow yet again. He condemned a movement against the king of Naples and uncovered the sale of indulgences for it, therefore ruining the priests' income. Indulgences were letters of pardon issued by the pope for sins, which permitted a person to get relief from temporal punishment for the payment of money. To not bring any problems to the city of Prague, he fled into the country. While in exile, he wrote the work On Simony, which made the folks well aware of the clergy's love of money, as well as their cohorts the secular authorities, who supported them as they soaked the poor of all they had. As was true of most reformers, in difficult times, they would depend on God's Word to lead the way, so Hus defended his position with, "Every faithful Christian should be so minded as not to hold anything contrary to the Holy Scriptures."

Hus shortly thereafter wrote an exposition entitled De Ecclesia (On the Church). Within the paper, he expressed a number of suggestions, one of which was the fact "That Peter never was, and is not, the head of the Church." Hus had determined from his exposition of Matthew 16:15-18 that it was not Peter, who was the foundation and head of the church; it was Jesus Christ, who filled that position. For Hus, the real authority belongs with the law of Christ, which was found in the Word of God, not man.

The Council of Constance

The rivalry had grown to the point where the Catholic Church could no longer sit by while Hus buried them in publication after publication, exposing their wrongdoing. They sent for him to come and answer for his views before the Council of Constance, held from 1414 to 1418 near Lake Constance. On December 4, 1414, the pope had delegated a committee of three bishops with an initial inquiry against Hus. The witnesses for the prosecution had their opportunity to speak, but Hus was not allowed a supporter for his defense. He continued to stand fast against the authority of the pope.

The council at one point asked Hus to withdraw his teachings, and he responded that he would if they could prove him wrong with Scripture, in accordance with 2 Timothy 3:14-16. Hus allowed his Christian conscience to lead the way and knew that he would never live with himself if he offered some vague retraction that might save face and save his life. He clearly stated, "My wish always has been that better doctrine be proved to me out of Scripture, and then I would be most ready to recant." He challenged the council to have their least member to show him from God's Word where he erred. They were not so inclined and condemned him as a heretic instead and him back to prison without anything being discussed from the Bible.

The condemnation of Hus took place on July 6, 1415; he was officially condemned in the cathedral of Constance. The bishop of Lodi delivered a discourse on the duty of eliminating heresy; then some theses of Hus and Wycliffe and a report of his trial were read. Hus objected several times

loudly, and when his appeal to Christ was rejected as a condemnable heresy, he exclaimed, "O God and Lord, now the council condemns even thine own act and thine own law as heresy, since thou thyself didst lay thy cause before thy Father as the just judge, as an example for us, whenever we are sorely oppressed."

John Hus had his priesthood publicly stripped from him, as well as having his writings burned in the churchyard. At some point, he was led out into a field and burned at the stake.

The Accomplishments of John Hus

The John Hus accomplishments at reform were 100 years before the start of the official Reformation, which was started by Martin Lither in 1517. John Hus and John Wycliffe were pioneers in opposing the pope and having their only true guide be that of the authority of Scripture. Hus helped to begin the commencement of the freedom of individuals, to allow their conscience to decide what is Scriptural and what is not.

In the early 1500s, Martin Luther was making a similar name for himself, as he was considered a Hussite. Obviously, we see Hus in his words, "Unless I am convicted by Scripture and plain reason—I do not accept the authority of popes and councils, for they have contradicted each other— my conscience is captive to the Word of God." Perhaps that is why he said: "We are all Hussites without knowing it."

John Hus, John Wycliffe, Martin Luther, and William Tyndale were the foundation of this return to Scripture, something that took the Reformation back to being like first-century Christianity. Of course, these ones did, not easily set the darkness of the period between the end of the Roman Empire in the fifth century and the early fifteenth-century, aside, as they were not able to shake off all the doctrines of tradition, but they established quite a few. Together, they reestablished the doctrine of *sola scriptura*, or Scripture alone, which means that Scripture, not popes or church councils, establishes all doctrinal matters. They returned to the Lord Jesus Christ, and early Christians enlightened view on this matter. – John 17:17; 18:37.

There is a battle that has been underway over the last 150-years between liberal Christianity and conservative Christianity, and it all boils down to the Bible. The liberal movement does not see the Bible as the Word of God, but instead, sees it as the word of men, filled with errors and contradictions, as well as myths and legends. The true conservative movement, on the other hand, sees the Bible as the Word of God, inspired and fully inerrant, the foundation of all they believe to be true.

Sadly, the liberal scholarship movement is at about 80 percent, with the conservative being around 20 percent. We are in a battle for the survival of the faith, and we too must take the same stand as that of John Hus, who echoed the words of the apostles, "We must obey God as ruler rather than men." – Acts 5:29.

CHAPTER 1 Anglo-Saxon Versions

Frederic G. Kenyon

Bruce Metzger writes,

In Britain, as elsewhere, missionary work proceeded almost entirely by means of the spoken word. Any translation of the Scriptures consisted of a free and extemporaneous rendering of the Latin text into the vernacular speech. Interlinear translations into Old English begin to appear in the ninth and tenth centuries. Among surviving copies of Anglo-Saxon renderings of the Gospels in various dialects are the famous Lindisfarne Gospels, a Latin manuscript (now in the British Library) written by Bishop Eadfrith of Lindisfarne toward the end of the seventh century. About the middle of the tenth century, a priest named Aldred wrote between the lines a literal rendering of the Latin in the Northumbrian dialect. A similar gloss is provided in the Rushworth worth Gospels, a manuscript copied from the Lindisfarne Gospels and now housed in the Bodleian Library, Oxford. The Rushworth glosses are practically transcripts of the Lindisfarne glosses so far as the Gospels of Mark, Luke, and John are concerned, but in Matthew the Rushworth gloss is an independent rendering in the rare Mercian dialect by a priest named Farman. A copy of the four Gospels in West Saxon orthography is preserved at Cambridge University Library and is generally dated to about A.D. 1050. According cording to an inscription, the manuscript was given by Bishop Le- ofric (d. 1072) to his cathedral church at Exeter. In addition to the four Gospels, the manuscript contains the apocryphal Gospel of Nicodemus and the Embassy of Nathan the Jew to Tiberius Caesar, both in Anglo-Saxon.

The Norman conquest of England (A.D. 1066) marked the end of the production of Scripture translation into Anglo-Saxon and Old English. For some three centuries, Norman French largely supplanted English among educated people; Latin, of course, continued to be used by the clergy. In the fourteenth century, English translation of parts of the Scriptures began to appear again, the form of the language being what is now called Middle English.[3]

The history of the English Bible begins early in the history of the English people, though not quite at the beginning of it, and only slowly attains to any magnitude. The Bible which was brought into the country by the first missionaries, by Aidan in the north and Augustine in the south, was the Latin Bible; and for some considerable time after the first preaching of Christianity to the English no vernacular version would be required. Nor is there any trace of a vernacular Bible in the Celtic Church, which still existed in Wales and Ireland. The literary language of the educated minority was Latin; and the instruction of the newly converted English tribes was carried on by oral teaching and preaching. As time went on, however, and monasteries were founded, many of whose inmates were imperfectly acquainted either with English or with Latin, a demand arose for English translations of the Scriptures. This took two forms. On the one hand, there was a call for word-for-word translations of the Latin, which might assist readers to a comprehension of the Latin Bible; and, on the other, for continuous versions or paraphrases, which might be read to, or by, those whose skill in reading Latin was small.

The earliest form, so far as is known, in which this demand was met was the poem of Caedmon, the work of a monk of Whitby in the third quarter of the seventh century, which gives a metrical paraphrase of parts of both testaments. The only extant manuscript of the poem (in the Bodleian) belongs to the end of the tenth century, and it is doubtful how much of it really goes back to the time of Caedmon. In any case, the poem as it appears here does not appear to be later than the eighth century. A tradition, originating with Bale, attributed an English version of the Psalms to Aldhelm, bishop of Sherborne (died 707), but it appears to be quite baseless, (See A.S. Cook, *Biblical Quotations in Old English Prose Writers*, 1878, pp. xiv-xviii). An Anglo-Saxon Psalter in an eleventh century manuscript at Paris (partly in prose and partly in verse) has been identified, without any evidence, with this imaginary work. The well-known story of the death of Bede (in 735) shows him engaged on an English translation of St. John's Gospel [one early manuscript (at St. Gall) represents this as extending only to John 6:9; but so abrupt a conclusion seems inconsistent with the course of the narrative], but of this all traces have disappeared. The scholarship of the monasteries of Wearmouth and Jarrow, which had an important influence on the textual history of the Latin Vulgate, did not concern itself with vernacular translations; and no further trace of an English

---

[3] Bruce Metzger. Bible in Translation, The: Ancient and English Versions (pp. 55-56). Kindle Edition.

Bible appears until the ninth century. To that period is assigned a word-for-word translation of the Psalter, written between the lines of a Latin manuscript (Cotton MS Vaspasian A.I., in the British Museum), which was the progenitor of several similar glosses between that date and the twelfth century; and to it certainly belongs the attempt of Alfred to educate his people by English translations of the works which he thought most needful to them. He is said to have undertaken a version of the Psalms, of which no portion survives, unless the prose portion (Psalms 1-50) of the above-mentioned Paris manuscript is a relic of it; but we still have the translation of the Decalogue, the summary of the Mosaic law, and the letter of the Council of Jerusalem (Acts 15:23-29), which he prefixed to his code of laws. To the tenth century belongs probably the verse portion of the Paris manuscript, and the interlinear translation of the Gospels in Northumbrian dialect inserted by the priest Aldred in the Lindisfarne Gospels (British Museum), which is repeated in the Rushworth Gospels (Bodleian) of the same century, with the difference that the version of Matthew is there in the Mercian dialect. This is the earliest extant translation of the Gospels into English.

The earliest independent version of any of the books of the Bible has likewise generally been assigned to the tenth century, but if this claim can be made good at all, it can apply only to the last years of that century. The version in question is a translation of the Gospels in the dialect of Wessex, of which six manuscripts (with a fragment of a seventh) are now extant. It was edited by W. Skeat, *The Holy Gospels in Anglo-Saxon* (1871-1877); two manuscripts are in the British Museum, two at Cambridge, and two (with a fragment of another) at Oxford. From the number of copies which still survive, it must be presumed to have had a certain circulation, at any rate in Wessex, and it continued to be copied for at least a century. The earliest manuscripts are assigned to the beginning of the eleventh century; but it is observable that Ælfric the Grammarian, abbot of Eynsham, writing about 990, says that the English at that time "had not the evangelical doctrines among their writings ... those books excepted which King Alfred wisely turned from Latin into English" [preface to Ælfric's *Homilies*, edited by B. Thorpe, London, 1843-46]. In a subsequent treatise (*Treatise Concerning the Old and New Testament*, ed. W. Lisle, London, 1623) also (the date of which is said to be about 1010, see Dietrich, *Zeitsch. f. hist. Theol.* 1856, quoted by Cook, *op. cit.*, p. lxiv.) he speaks as if no English version of the Gospels were in existence, and refers his readers to his own homilies on the Gospels. Since Ælfric had been a monk at Winchester and abbot of Cerne, in Dorset, it is difficult to understand how he could have failed to know of the Wessex version of the Gospels, if it had been produced and circulated much before 1000; and it seems probable that it only came into existence early in the eleventh century. In this case it was contemporaneous with another work of translation, due to Ælfric himelf. Ælfric, at the request of Æthelweard, son of his patron Æthelmær, ealdorman of Devonshire and founder of Eynsham Abbey, produced a paraphrase of the Heptateuch, homilies containing epitomes of the Books of Kings and Job, and brief versions of Esther, Judith, and Maccabees. These have the interest of being the earliest extant English version of the narrative books of the Old Testament. [The Heptateuch and Job were printed by E. Thwaites (Oxford, 1698). For the rest, see Cook, *op. cit.*]

CHAPTER 2 Middle English Bible Version and John Wycliffe

Frederic G. Kenyon

The Norman Conquest checked for a time all the vernacular literature of England, including the translations of the Bible. One of the first signs of its revival was the production of the *Ormulum*, a poem which embodies metrical versions of the Gospels and Acts, written about the end of the twelfth century. The main biblical literature of this period, however, was French. For the benefit of the Norman settlers in England, translations of the greater part of both Old Testament and New Testament were produced during the twelfth and thirteenth centuries. Especially notable among these was the version of the Apocalypse, because it was frequently accompanied by a series of illustrations, the best examples of which are the finest (and also the most quaint) artistic productions of the period in the sphere of book-illustration. Nearly 90 manuscripts of this version are known, ranging from the first half of the twelfth century to the first half of the fifteenth [see P. Berger, *La Bible Francaise au moyen age*, p. 78 ff.; L. Delisle and P. Meyer, *L'Apocalypse en Francais* (Paris, 1901); and *New Paleographical Society*, part 2, plates 38, 39], some having been produced in England, and others in France; and in the fourteenth century it reappears in an English dress, having been translated apparently about that time. This English version (which at one time was attributed to Wycliffe) is known in no less than 16 manuscripts, which fall into at least two classes [see Miss A.C. Paues, *A Fourteenth-Century English Biblical Version* (Cambridge, 1902), pp. 24-30]; and it is noteworthy that from the second of these was derived the version which appears in the revised Wycliffite Bible, to be mentioned presently.

The fourteenth century, which saw the practical extinction of the general use of the French language in England, and the rise of a real vernacular literature, saw also a great revival of vernacular Biblical literature, beginning apparently with the Book of Psalms. Two English versions of the Psalter were produced at this period, one of which enjoyed great popularity. This was the work of Richard Rolle, hermit of Hampole, in Yorkshire (*d.*1349). It contains the Latin text of the Psalter, followed verse by verse by an English translation and commentary. Originally written in the northern dialect, it soon spread over all England, and many manuscripts of it still exist in which the dialect has been altered to suit southern tastes. Towards the end of the century Rolle's work suffered further change, the commentary being re-written from a strongly Lollard point of view, and in this shape, it continued to circulate far into the sixteenth century. Another version of the Psalter was produced contemporaneously with Rolle's, somewhere in the West Midlands. The authorship of it was formerly attributed to William of Shoreham, vicar of Chart Sutton, in Kent, but for no other reason than that in one of the two manuscripts in which it is preserved (Brit. Mus. Add. MS 17376), the other being at Trinity College, Dublin) it is now bound up with his religious poems. The dialect, however, proves that this authorship is impossible, and the version must be put down as anonymous. As in the case of Rolle's translation, the Latin and English texts are intermixed, verse by verse; but there is no commentary. [See K.S. Bulbring, *The Earliest Complete English Prose Psalter* (Early English Text Society), 1891).]

The Psalter was not the only part of the Bible of which versions came into existence in the course of the fourteenth century. At Magdalene College, Cambridge (Pepys MS 2498), is an English narrative of the life of Christ, compiled out of a re-arrangement of the Gospels for Sundays and holy days throughout the year. Quite recently, too, a group of manuscripts, which (so far as they were known at all) had been regarded as belonging to the Wycliffite Bible, has been shown by Miss Anna C. Paues [*A Fourteenth-Century English Biblical Version* (Cambridge, 1902)] to contain an independent translation of the New Testament. It is not complete, the Gospels being represented only by Matthew 1:1 to 6:8, and the Apocalypse being altogether omitted. The original nucleus seems, indeed, to have consisted of the four larger Catholic Epistles and the Epistles of St. Paul, to which were subsequently added 2 and 3 John, Jude, Acts, and Matthew 1:1-6:8. Four manuscripts of this version are at present known, the oldest being one at Selwyn College, Cambridge, which was written about 1400. The prologue narrates that the translation was made at the request of a monk and a nun by their superior, who defers to their earnest desire, although, as he says, it is at the risk of his life. This phrase seems to show that the work was produced after the rise of the great party controversy which is associated with the name of Wycliffe.

John Wycliffe

With Wycliffe (1320-1384) we reach a landmark in the history of the English Bible, in the production of the first complete version of both the Old Testament and the New Testament. It belongs to the last period of Wycliffe's life, that in which he was engaged in open war with the Papacy and with most of the official chiefs of the English Church. It was connected with his institution of "poor priests," or mission preachers, and formed part of his scheme of appealing to the populace in general against the doctrines and supremacy of Rome. The New Testament seems to have been completed about 1380, the Old Testament between 1382 and 1384. Exactly how much of it was done by Wyclif's own hand is uncertain. The greater part of the Old Testament (as far as Baruch 3:20) is assigned in an Oxford manuscript to Nicholas Hereford, one of Wyclif's principal supporters at that university; and it is certain that this part of the translation is in a different style (more stiff and pedantic) from the rest. The New Testament is generally attributed to Wyclif himself, and he may also have completed the Old Testament, which Hereford apparently had to abandon abruptly, perhaps when he was summoned to London and excommunicated in 1382. This part of the work is free and vigorous in style, though its interpretation of the original is often strange, and many sentences in it can have conveyed very little idea of their meaning to its readers. Such as it was, however, it was a complete English Bible, addressed to the whole English people, high and low, rich and poor. That this is the case is proved by the character of the copies which have survived (about 30 in number). Some are large folio volumes, handsomely written and illuminated in the best, or nearly the best, style of the period; such is the fine copy, in two volumes (now Brit. Mus. Egerton MSS 617, 618), which once belonged to Thomas, Duke of Gloucester, uncle of Richard II. Others are plain copies of ordinary size, intended for private persons or monastic libraries; for it is clear that, in spite of official disfavor and eventual prohibition, there were many places in England where Wyclif and his Bible were welcomed. Wyclif, indeed, enjoyed advantages from personal repute and influential support such as had been enjoyed by no English translator since Alfred. An Oxford scholar, at one time Master of Balliol, holder of livings successively from his college and the Crown, employed officially on behalf of his country in controversy with the Pope, the friend and protege of John of Gaunt and other prominent nobles, and enjoying as a rule the strenuous support of the University of Oxford, Wyclif was in all respects a person of weight and influence in the realm, who could not be silenced or isolated by the opposition of bishops such as Arundel. The work that he had done had struck its roots too deep to be destroyed, and though it was identified with Lollardism by its adversaries, its range was much wider than that of anyone sect or party.

Wycliffe's translation, however, though too strong to be overthrown by its opponents, was capable of improvement by its friends. The difference of style between Hereford and his continuator or continuators, the stiff and unpopular character of the work of the former, and the imperfections inevitable in a first attempt on so large a scale, called aloud for revision; and a second Wycliffite Bible, the result of a very complete revision of its predecessor, saw the light not many years after the reformer's death. The authorship of the second version is doubtful. It was assigned by Forshall and Madden, the editors of the Wycliffite Bible, to John Purvey, one of Wycliffe's most intimate followers; but the evidence is purely circumstantial, and rests mainly on verbal resemblances between the translator's preface and known works of Purvey, together with the fact that a copy of this preface is found attached to a copy of the earlier version which was once Purvey's property. What is certain is that the second version is based upon the first and that the translator's preface is permeated with Wycliffite opinions. This version speedily superseded the other, and in spite of a decree passed, at Arundel's instigation, by the council of Blackfriars in 1408, it must have circulated in large numbers. Over 140 copies are still in existence, many of them small pocket volumes such as must have been the personal property of private individuals for their own study. Others belonged to the greatest personages in the land, and copies are still in existence which formerly had for owners Henry VI, Henry VII, Edward VI, and Elizabeth.

With the production of the second Wycliffite version the history of the manuscript, the English Bible comes to an end. Purvey's work was on the level of the best scholarship and textual knowledge of the age, and it satisfied the requirements of those who needed a vernacular Bible. That it did not reach modern standards in these respects goes without saying. In the first place, it was translated from the Latin Vulgate, not from the original Hebrew and Greek, with which there is no reason to suppose that Wycliffe or his assistants were familiar. Secondly, its exegesis is often deficient, and some passages in it must have been wholly unintelligible to its readers. This, however, may be said even of some parts of the AV, so that it is a small reproach to Wycliffe and Purvey; and on the whole, it is a straightforward and intelligible version of the Scriptures. A few examples of this, the first complete English Bible, and the first version in which the English approaches sufficiently near to its modern form to be generally intelligible may be given here.

John 14:1-7. Be not youre herte affraied, ne drede it. Ye bileuen in god, and bileue ye in me. In the hous of my fadir ben many dwellyngis: if ony thing lasse I hadde seid to you, for I go to make redi to you a place. And if I go and make redi to you a place, eftsone I come and I schal take you to my silf, that where I am, ye be. And whidir I go ye witen: and ye witen the wey. Thomas seith to him, Lord, we witen not whidir thou goist, and hou moun we wite the weie. Ihesus seith to him, I am weye truthe and liif: no man cometh to the fadir, but bi me. If ye hadden knowe me, sothli ye hadden knowe also my fadir: and aftirwarde ye schuln knowe him, and ye han seen hym.

2 Cor. 1:17-20. But whanne I wolde this thing, whether I uside unstidfastnesse? ether tho thingis that I thenke, I thenke aftir the fleische, that at me be it is and it is not. But god is trewe, for oure word that was at you, is and is not, is not thereinne, but is in it. Forwhi ihesus crist the sone of god, which is prechid among you bi us, bi me and siluan and tymothe, ther was not in hym is and is not, but is was in hym. Forwhi hou many euer ben biheestis of god, in thilke is ben fulfillid. And therfor and bi him we seien Amen to god, to oure glorie.

Ephesians 3:14-21. For grace of this thing I bowe my knees to the fadir of oure lord ihesus crist, of whom eche fadirheed in heuenes and in erthe is named, that he geue to you aftir the richessis of his glorie, vertu to be strengthid bi his spirit in the ynner man; that criste dwelle bi feith in youre hertis; that ye rootid and groundid in charite, moun comprehende with alle seyntis whiche is the breede and the lengthe and the highist and the depnesse; also to wite the charite of crist more excellent thanne science, that ye be fillid in all the plente of god. And to hym that is myghti to do alle thingis more plenteuousli thanne we axen, or undirstande bi the vertu that worchith in us, to hym be glorie in the chirche and in crist ihesus in to alle the generaciouns of the worldis. Amen.

The English manuscript Bible was now complete, and no further translation was issued in this form. The Lollard controversy died down amid the strain of the French wars and the passions of the wars of the Roses; and when, in the sixteenth century, religious questions once more came to the front, the situation had been fundamentally changed through the invention of printing. The first book that issued from the press was the Latin Bible (popularly known as the Mazarin Bible), published by Fust and Gutenberg in 1456. For the Latin Bible (the form in which the Scriptures had hitherto been mainly known in Western Europe) there was indeed so great a demand, that no less than 124 editions of it are said to have been issued before the end of the fifteenth century; but it was only slowly that scholars realized the importance of utilizing the printing press for the circulation of the Scriptures, either in their original tongues, or in the vernaculars of Europe. The Hebrew Psalter was printed in 1477, the complete Old Testament in 1488. The Greek Bible, both Old Testament and New Testament, was included in the great Complutensian Polyglot of Cardinal Ximenes, printed in 1514-17, but not published till 1522. The Greek New Testament (edited by Erasmus) was first published by Froben in 1516, the Old Testament by the Aldine press in 1518. In the way of vernacular versions, a French Bible was printed at Lyons about 1478, and another about 1487; a Spanish Pentateuch was printed (by Jews) in 1497; a German Bible was printed at Strassburg by Mentelin in 1466, and was followed by eighteen others (besides many Psalters and other separate books) between that date and 1522, when the first portion of Luther's translation appeared. In England, Caxton inserted the main part of the Old Testament narrative in his translation of the *Golden Legend* (which in its original form already contained the Gospel story), published in 1483; but no regular English version of the Bible was printed until 1525, with which date a new chapter in the history of the English Bible begins.

CHAPTER 3 The Wycliffe Bible

Edward D. Andrews

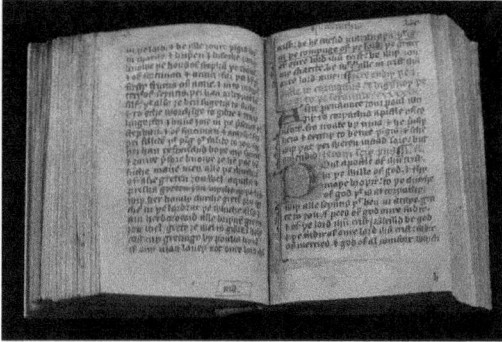

While the Wycliffe Bible is not the first English Bible, it is the first complete English Bible. It came to us through the efforts and influence of John Wycliffe (c. 1330-1384), a Catholic priest and a professor of theology at Oxford, England, called the "morning star of the Reformation" because of the religious principles that he developed through his investigation of Scripture and witnessed about, a great risk to himself. In his treatise of 1378, De Potestate Papae ("Concerning the Authority of the Pope"), Wycliffe was above all open and candid when it came to the church's disregard in teaching the Bible, the timeless "exemplar" of the Christian religion, was the single standard of doctrine, to which no church authority might legitimately add, and that the authority of the pope was unreliable in Scripture.

Wycliffe once declared: "Would to God that every parish church in this land had a good Bible and good expositions on the gospel, and that the priests studied them well, and taught truly the gospel and God's commands to the people!"[4] Wycliffe viewed the Bible as the Word of God, penned to every person. Therefore, he felt personally obligated to render the Scriptures in a translation that the layperson-churchgoer would have access to its truths. Wycliffe was mindful of the mistreatments in the church, which he wrote and preached against, such as bribery in the monastic orders, papal taxation, the doctrine of transubstantiation (the claim that the bread and wine used in the Mass literally change into the body and blood of Jesus Christ), the confession, and church involvement in everyday life. Wycliffe had influential enemies who were finally able to bring him to trial for heresy. Twenty-four theses from his writings and sermons were condemned as heretical or erroneous at a synod held at Blackfriars, London, on May 21, 1382.

---

[4] Writings of the Reverend and learned John Wickliff - Page 125

It is uncertain whether Wycliffe himself actually worked directly on the translation that bears his name. He died in peace on the last day of 1384 at Lutterworth. However, it is his translation, and rightfully bears his name, the Wycliffe Bible, for if it were not for his inspiration and influence, the translation would have never gotten done. To this end, Wycliffe, in the last years of his life, embarked on the task of translating the Latin Vulgate Bible into English, with the help of his associates, John Purvey and Nicholas of Hereford, two complete versions of the Scriptures were produced. The 1382 version was an extremely literal translation, following the Latin word for word, even violating the English word order. The 1388 version was less literal and more in line the English idiom of his time. Because the translation was made from the Latin Vulgate text, it also included the Old Testament apocryphal and deuterocanonical books.

Principles of Bible Translation

Purvey set down some principles of Bible translation:

> First, it is to be known that the best translating out of Latin into English is to translate after the sentence and not only after the words, so the sentence be as open or opener, in English as in Latin, and go not far from the letter; and if the letter may not be followed in the translating, let the sentence be ever whole and open, for the words ought to serve the intent and sentence, or else the words be superfluous or false.[5]

Some have been so bold as to use this statement, to suggest that Wycliffe and his associates supported some dynamic equivalent translation philosophy.[6] Well, this certainly could not be further from the truth.

> Furthermore, since the charge of naivete is in part an attempt to marginalize adherents of essentially literal translation as an inconsequential segment of the English translation scene, it is important to set the record straight in this regard. Even though new English translations have been dominated by dynamic equivalence, the English Bibles actually in use have been pretty evenly divided between literal and free translations. And in terms of the

---

[5] F. F. Bruce, *The English Bible: A History of Translations* (New York: Oxford Univ. Press, 1961), 19–20.

[6] Strauss, Mark L.; Scorgie, Glen G.; Voth, Steven M.: *The Challenge of Bible Translation: Communicating God's Word to the World.* Zondervan, p. 201.

history of English Bible translation, dynamic equivalence is almost wholly a modern phenomenon. No major English translation was dominated by dynamic equivalence until the mid-twentieth century, and in this regard appeals to the Wycliffe translation of the fourteenth century and occasional freedoms that Tyndale took are irrelevant to the discourse. If Tyndale gave us anomalies like claiming that Paul sailed from Philippi after the Easter holidays, he also coined words like intercession and atonement in order to express the theological con-tent of the original. In terms of the history of English Bible translation, therefore, essentially literal translation is the dominant tradition, not a lightweight view held by a few ignorant people.[7]

The Council of Constance condemned **John Hus** as a heretic, the Bohemian (Czech), who had been influenced by John Wycliffe. Hus refused to recant and was burned to death at the stake in 1415. The same council also ordered that the bones of Wycliffe be dug up and burned although he had been dead and buried for over 30 years! The Wycliffe Bible was condemned and burned as well. Both assistants of Wycliffe, Purvey, and Nicholas would be jailed. They were tortured until they recanted their teachings. Then, in 1428, an outlandish and appalling event occurred. Because Pope Martin V insisted, the grave of John Wycliffe was broken open in accordance with the decree of the Council of Constance made 14 years earlier. His remains were dug up and burned, and the ashes were taken down to the little river Swift a short distance away. However, as the ashes of Wycliffe were carried far and wide by the river, so too was his message throughout the next few centuries.

In 1407 the synod of clergy called in Oxford, England, by Archbishop Thomas Arundel explicitly prohibited the translating of the Bible into English or any other modern tongue.[8] In 1431, also in England, Bishop Stafford of Wells banned the translating of the Bible into English and the possessing of such translations.[9] In spite of this misplaced religious fervor, about 180 copies of the Wycliffe Bible in whole or in part have survived, largely dating prior to 1450. Of these, there are 15 copies of the Old Testament and 18 copies of the New Testament, which are of the 1382 more literal version. Many speak of the influence that Martin Luther's

---

[7] Grudem, Wayne; Packer, J. I.: *Translating Truth: The Case for Essentially Literal Bible Translation.* Good News Publishers/Crossway Books, p. 63.

[8] The Lollard Bible and Other Medieval Biblical Versions, by Margaret Deanesly, 1920, p. 24.

[9] The Lollard Bible, p. 227.

version had on the German language, yet the Wycliffe Bible had no less of an effect on the English people and the English language.

The death of John Wycliffe caused great elation amongst his adversaries. They would no longer be inundated by the difficulties that his teachings had brought about. They would be able to rebuild their grasp over the people. Wycliffe's writings and his Bible translation into English could be destroyed, and be out of sight and thus out of mind. Although that may have been their expectation, it did not happen the way that they had hoped. Wycliffe's followers, the Lollards, were more resolute than ever to keep his work alive. Wycliffe's writings and portions of the Bible were circulated all over England by a group of preachers frequently referred to as "Poor Priests" for the reason that they went about in simple clothing, barefoot, and without material belongings. They were also mockingly called Lollards, from the Middle Dutch word Lollaerd, or "one who mumbles prayers or hymns."[10] The survival of so many Wycliffe Bibles in the face of such opposition is evidence of the persistence and effectiveness of the courageous Bible preachers: the Lollards![11]

Bruce Metzger informs us in his *The Bible in Translation* that, "during the first half of the fifteenth century, some copies of this version were augmented by the inclusion following Colossians of the spurious Letter of Paul to the Laodicean's. In Colossians 4:16, Paul directs the Colossians, after they have read his letter to them, to pass it on to the church of Laodicea and to see that they, in turn, have an opportunity to "read also the letter from Laodicea." Although no such letter occurs in the New Testament, before the end of the fourth century someone forged such a composition in Paul's name. This inauthentic letter circulated in Latin for many centuries and sometimes was included in manuscripts of the Latin Vulgate."[12]

---

[10] Inc Merriam-Webster, Merriam-Webster's Collegiate Dictionary., Eleventh ed. (Springfield, Mass.: Merriam-Webster, Inc., 2003).

[11] The complete Wycliffe Bible did not appear in a printed edition of until 1850, when Josiah Forshall and Frederic Madden distributed the earlier and the later versions, printed side by side in four volumes (Oxford University Press).

[12] Bruce Metzger. The Bible in Translation, Ancient and English Versions (p. 58).

CHAPTER 4 Dutch Bible and Textual Scholar Erasmus of Rotterdam

Edward D. Andrews

It is really difficult to enter into this next era of the English Bibles without talking about Desiderius Erasmus and the Textus Receptus (Received Text) that would impact English Translations for centuries to come.

> I WOULD have these words translated into all languages, so that not only Scots and Irish, but Turks and Saracens too might read them . . . I long for the ploughboy to sing them to himself as he follows his plough, the weaver to hum them to the tune of his shuttle, the traveler to beguile with them the dullness of his journey. (Clayton 2006, 230)

Dutch scholar Desiderius Erasmus penned those words in the early part of the 16th century. Like his English counterpart, William Tyndale, it was his greatest desire that God's Word is widely translated and that even the plowboy would have access to it.

Much time has passed since the Reformation, and 98 percent of the world we live in today has access to the Bible. There is little wonder that the Bible has become the bestseller of all time. It has influenced men from all walks of life to fight for freedom and truth. This is especially true during the Reformation of Europe throughout the 16th century. These leading men were of great faith, courage, and strength, such as Martin Luther, William Tyndale, while others, like Erasmus, was more subtle in the change that he produced. Thus, it has been said of the Reformation that Martin Luther only opened the door to it after Erasmus picked the lock.

There is not one historian of the period, who would deny that Erasmus was a great scholar. Remarking on his character, the *Catholic Encyclopedia* says: "He had an unequaled talent for form, great journalistic gifts, a surpassing power of expression: for strong and moving discourse, keen irony, and covert sarcasm, he was unsurpassed." (Vol. 5, p. 514) Consequently, when Erasmus went to see Sir Thomas More, the Lord Chancellor of England, just before Erasmus made himself known, More was so impressed with his exchange that he shortly said: "You are either Erasmus or the Devil."

The wit of Erasmus was evidenced in a response that he gave to Frederick, elector of Saxony, who asked him what he thought about Martin

Luther. Erasmus retorted, "Luther has committed two blunders; he has ventured to touch the crown of the pope and the bellies of the monks." (*Cyclopedia of Biblical, Theological, and Ecclesiastical Literature*: Vol. 3 – p, 279) However, we must ask what type of influence did the Bible have on Erasmus and, in turn, what did he do to affect its future? First, let us look at the early years of Erasmus' life.

Erasmus' Early Life

He was born in Rotterdam, the Netherlands, in 1466. He was not a happy boy living in a home as the illegitimate son of a Dutch priest. He was faced with the double tragedy of his mother's death at seventeen, and his father shortly thereafter. His guardians ignored his desire to enter the university; rather they sent him to the Augustinian monastery of Steyn. Erasmus gained a vast knowledge of the Latin language, the classic as well as the Church Fathers. In time, this type of life was so detestable to him; he jumped on the opportunity, at the age of twenty-six, to become secretary to the bishop of Cambrai, Henry of Bergen, in France. This afforded him his chance to enter university studies in Paris. However, he was a sickly man, always ill, suffering from poor health throughout his entire life.

It was in 1499 that Erasmus was invited to visit England. It was here that he met Thomas More, John Colet and other theologians in London, which fortified his resolution to apply himself to Biblical studies. In order to understand the Bible's message better, he applied himself more fully in his study of Greek, soon being able to teach it to others. It was around this time that Erasmus penned a treatise entitled Handbook of the Christian Soldier, in which he advised the young Christian to study the Bible, saying: "There is nothing that you can believe with greater certitude than what you read in these writings." (Erasmus and Dolan 1983, 37)

While trying to escape the plague, make a living in an economy that had bottomed worse than our 20th century Great Depression, Erasmus found himself at Louvain, Belgium, in 1504. It was here that he fell in love with the study of textual criticism while visiting the Monastery of Parc. Within the library, Erasmus discovered a manuscript of Italian scholar Lorenzo Valla: *Annotations on the New Testament*. Textual criticism is an art and science that studies manuscripts, evaluating internal and external evidence, especially of the Bible or works of literature, in order to determine which readings are the original or most authentic. Erasmus had commissioned himself toward the task of restoring the original text of the Greek New Testament.

Erasmus moved on to Italy and subsequently pushed on to England once again. It is this trip that brought to mind his original meeting with Thomas More, meditating on the origin of More's name (*moros*, Greek for "a fool"); he penned a write or satire, which he called Praise of Folly. In this work, Erasmus takes the abstract quality "folly" as being a human being and pictured it as encroaching in all aspects of life, but nowhere is folly more in obvious than amid the theologians and clergy. This is his subtle way of exposing the abuses of the clergy. It is these abuses, which had brought on the Reformation that was now festering. "As to the popes," he wrote, "if they claim to be the successors of the Apostles, they should consider that the same things are required of them as were practiced by their predecessors." Instead of doing this, he perceived, they believe that "to teach the people is too laborious; to interpret the scripture is to invade the prerogative of the schoolmen; to pray is too idle." There is little wonder that it was said of Erasmus that he had "a surpassing power of expression"! (Nichols 2006, Vol. 2, 6)

The First Greek Text

Whilst teaching Greek at Cambridge University in England, Erasmus continued with his work of revising the text of the Greek New Testament. One of his friends, Martin Dorpius, attempted to persuade him that the Latin did not need to be corrected from the Greek. Dorpius makes the same error in thinking that the "King James Only" people make, arguing: "For is it likely that the whole Catholic Church would have erred for so many centuries, seeing that she has always used and sanctioned this translation? Is it probable that so many holy fathers, so many consummate scholars would have longed to convey a warning to a friend?" (Campbell 1949, 71) Thomas More joined Erasmus in replying to these arguments, making the point that the importance lies within having an accurate text in the original languages.

In Basel, Switzerland, Erasmus was about to be hassled by the printer Johannes Froben. Froben was alerted that Cardinal Ximenes of Toledo, Spain, had been putting together a Greek and Latin Testament in 1514. However, he was delaying publication until he had the whole Bible completed. The first printed Greek critical text would have set the standard, with the other being all but ignored. Erasmus published his first edition in 1516, while the Complutensian Polyglot (many languages) was not issued until 1522

The fact that Erasmus was rushed to no end resulted in a Greek text that contained hundreds of typographical errors alone.[1] Textual scholar

Scrivener once stated: '[It] is in that respect the most faulty book I know,' (Scrivener 1894, 185) This comment does not even take into consideration the blatant interpolations (insert readings) into the text that were not part of the original. Erasmus was not lost to the typographical errors, which corrected a good many in later editions. This did not include the textual errors. It was his second edition of 1519 that was used by Martin Luther in his German translation and William Tyndale's English translation. This is exactly what Erasmus wanted, writing the following in that edition's preface: "I would have these words translated into all languages. . . . I long for the ploughboy to sing them to himself as he follows his plough."

Sadly, the continuous reproduction of this debased Greek New Testament, gave rise to it becoming the standard, being called the Textus Receptus (Received Text), taking over 400 years before it was dethroned by the critical Text of B. F. Westcott and F. J. A. Hort in 1881. Regardless of its imperfection, the Erasmus critical edition began the all-important work of textual criticism, which has only brought about a better critical text, as well as more accurate Bible translations.

As was true with many other early Bibles in the early days of the Reformation, it had its detractors. Like the Geneva Bible, but on a much tamer note, Erasmus was critical of the clergy in his notes. For instance, the text of Matthew 16:18, which says, "Thou art Peter, and upon this rock I will build my church." (Douay) Very plainly, he rejects the idea that this text is applied to primacy Peter, and that the pope is a successor of such. Imagine writing such a thing in the very edition you are going to dedicate to the pope! We can certainly see why Erasmus' works were prohibited, even in the universities.

Erasmus was not only concerned with ascertaining the original words; he was just as concerned with achieving an accurate understanding of those words. In 1519, he penned Principles of True Theology (shortened to The Ratio). Herein he introduces his principles for Bible study, his interpretation rules. Among them is the thought of never taking a quotation out of its context nor out of the line of thought of its author. Erasmus saw the Bible as a whole work by one author, and it should interpret itself.

Erasmus Contrasted with Luther

Erasmus penned a treatise called Familiar Colloquies in 1518, where again he was exposing the corruptions on the Church and the monasteries. Just one year earlier, in 1517, Martin Luther had nailed his 95 theses on the church door at Wittenberg, denouncing the indulgences, the scandal that had rocked numerous countries. Many folks were likely thinking that these two could bring change and reform. This was not going to be a team effort, though, as they both were at opposite ends of the spectrum on how to bring this reform about. Luther would come to condemn Erasmus, because he was viewed as being too moderate, seeking to make change peacefully within the Church. Many have viewed it as Erasmus thinking and writing, while Luther appeared to go beyond that with his actions.

The seemingly small bond they may have shared (by way of their writings against the Church establishment), was torn down the middle in 1524 when Erasmus penned the essay On the Freedom of the Will. Luther believed that salvation results from "justification by faith alone" (Latin, sola fide) and not from priestly absolution or works of penance. In fact, Luther was so adamant on his belief of "justification by faith alone" that in his Bible translation, he added the word "alone" to Romans 3:28. What Luther failed to understand was that Paul was writing about the works of the Mosaic Law. (Romans 3:19, 20, 28) Thus, Luther denied the notion that man possesses a free will. However, Erasmus would not accept such faulty reasoning, in that it would make God unjust because this would suggest that man would be unable to act in such a way as to affect his salvation.

As the Reformation was growing throughout Europe, Erasmus saw complaints from both sides. Many of the religious leaders who supported the reform movement chose to leave the Catholic Church. While they could not predict the result of their decision, they moved forward, many ending in death. This would not be true of Erasmus though, for he withdrew from the debate, yet he did refuse to be made cardinal. His approach was to try to appease both sides. Thus, Rome saw his writings as being that of a heretic, prohibiting them, while the reformers denounced him as refusing to risk his life for the cause. Here was a man, emotionally broken over criticism, but in fear of rocking the boat with Rome, so he cautiously sat on the sideline.

The affairs of Erasmus to the Reformation can be summarized as follows: "He was a reformer until the Reformation became a fearful reality; a jester at the bulwarks of the papacy until they began to give way; a propagator of the Scriptures until men betook themselves to the study and the application of them; depreciating the mere outward forms of religion until they had come to be estimated at their real value; in short, a learned, ingenious, benevolent, amiable, timid, irresolute man, who, bearing the responsibility, resigned to others the glory of rescuing the human mind from the bondage of a thousand years. The distance between his career and that of Luther was therefore continually enlarging, until they at length moved in opposite directions, and met each other with mutual animosity."—(McClintock and Strong 1894, 278).

The greatest gain from the Reformation is that the common person can now hold God's Word in his hand. In fact, the Englishperson has over 100 different translations from which to choose. From these 16th-century life and death struggles, in which Erasmus shared, there has materialized dependable and accurate Bible translations. Consequently, the 'plowboy' of 98 percent of the world can pick up his Bible, or at least part of it.

The Textus Receptus

The Dark Ages (5th to 15th centuries C.E.), was a time when the Church had the Bible locked up in the Latin language, and scholarship and learning were nearly nonexistent. However, with the birth of the Morning Star of the Reformation, John Wycliffe (1328-1384), and more officially in the 16th century Reformation, and the invention of the printing press in 1455, the restraints were loosened, and there was a rebirth of interest in the Greek language. Moreover, with the fall of Constantinople to the Turks 1453 C. E., many Greek scholars and their manuscripts were scattered abroad, resulting in a revival of Greek in the Western citadels of learning.

About fifty years later, or at the beginning of the sixteenth century, Ximenes, archbishop of Toledo, Spain, a man of rare capability and honor, invited foremost scholars of his land to his university at Alcala to produce a multiple-language Bible, not for the common people, but for the educated. The outcome would be the Polyglot, named Complutensian corresponding to the Latin of Alcala. This would be a Bible of six large volumes, beautifully bound, containing the Old Testament in four languages (Hebrew, Aramaic, Greek, and Latin) and the New Testament in two (Greek and Latin). For the Greek New Testament, these scholars had only a few manuscripts available to them, and those of late origin. One may wonder why this was the case when they were supposed to have access to the Vatican library. This Bible was completed in 1514, providing the first printed Greek New Testament, but did not receive approval by the pope to be published until 1520 and was not released to the public until 1522.

Froben, a printer in Basel, Switzerland became aware of the completion of the Complutensian Polyglot Bible and of its pending consent by the pope to be published. Immediately, he saw a prospect of making profits. He at once sent word to the Dutch scholar Desiderius Erasmus (1469-1536), who was the foremost European scholar of the day and whose works he had published in Latin, beseeching him to hurry through a Greek New Testament text. In an attempt to bring the first published Greek text to completion, Erasmus was only able to locate, in July of 1515, a few late cursive manuscripts for collating and preparing his text. It would go to press in October of 1515 and would be completed by March of 1516. In fact, Erasmus was in such a hurried mode he rushed the manuscript containing the Gospels to the printer without first editing it, making such changes, as he felt was necessary on the proof sheets. Because of this great rush job, this work also contained hundreds of typographical errors. Erasmus himself admitted this in its preface that it was "rushed through rather than edited." Bruce Metzger referred to the Erasmian text as a "debased form of the Greek Testament." (B. M. Metzger 1964, 1968, 1992, 103)

Needless to say, Erasmus was moved to produce an improved text in four succeeding editions of 1519, 1522, 1527, and 1535. Erasmus' editions of the Greek text, we are informed, ended up being an excellent achievement, a literary sensation. They were inexpensive, and the first two editions totaled 3,300 copies, in comparison to the 600 copies of the large and expensive six-volume Polyglot Bible. In the preface to his first edition, Erasmus stated, "I vehemently dissent from those who would not have private persons read the Holy Scriptures, nor have them translated into the vulgar tongues." (Baer 2007, 268)

Except for everyday practical consideration, the editions of Erasmus had little to vouch for them, for he had access to five (some say eight) Greek manuscripts of reasonably late origin and none of these were of the whole Greek New Testament. Rather, these comprised one or more sections into which the Greek texts were normally divided: (1) the Gospels; (2) Acts and the general epistles (James through Jude); (3) the letters of Paul; (4) Revelation. In fact, of the 5,800 Greek New Testament manuscripts that we now have, only about fifty are complete.

Consequently, Erasmus had but one copy of Revelation (twelfth century). Since it was incomplete, he merely retranslated the missing last six verses of the book from the Latin Vulgate back into Greek. He even frequently brought his Greek text in line with the Latin Vulgate; this is why there are some twenty readings in his Greek text not found in any other Greek manuscript.

Martin Luther would use Erasmus' 1519 edition for his German translation, and William Tyndale would use the 1522 edition for his English translation. Erasmus' editions were also the foundation for further Greek editions of the New Testament by others. For instance, the four published by Robert Estienne (Stephanus, 1503-59). According to Bruce Metzger, the third of these, published by Stephanus, in 1550, became the Textus Receptus or Received Text of Britain and the basis of the King James Version. This took place through Theodore de Beza (1519-1605), whose work was based on the corrupted third and fourth editions of the Erasmian text. Beza would produce nine editions of the Greek text, four being independent (1565, 1589, 1588-9, 1598), and the other five smaller reprints. It would be two of Beza's editions, that of 1589 and 1598, which would become the English Received Text.

Beza's Greek edition of the New Testament did not even differ as much as might be expected from those of Erasmus. Why do I say, as might be expected? Beza was a friend of the Protestant reformer, John Calvin, succeeding him at Geneva, and was also a well-known classical and biblical scholar. In addition, Beza possessed two important Greek manuscripts of the fourth and fifth century, the **D** and **D**ᵖ (also known as **D²**), the former of which contains most of the Gospels and Acts, as well as a fragment of 3 John and the latter containing the Pauline epistles. The Dutch Elzevir editions followed next, which were virtually identical to those of the Erasmian-influenced Beza text. It was in the second of seven of these, published in 1633, that there appeared the statement in the preface (in Latin): "You therefore now have the text accepted by everybody, in which we give nothing changed or corrupted." On the continent, this edition became the Textus Receptus or the Received Text. It seems that this success was in no small way due to the beauty and useful size of the Elzevir editions.

In Chapter 2, we will take a moment to look at how and what made the King James Bible so popular that it would be the bestselling Bible for four hundred years. It became so popular that the translation itself became venerated. How did the 1611 King James Version, attain a unique place in the hearts and minds of the English-speaking people?

CHAPTER 5 William Tyndale's Bible for the People

Frederic G. Kenyon

William Tyndale (c. 1490-1536) devoted himself early to Scripture studies, and by the time he had reached the age of about thirty he had taken for the work of his life the translation of the Bible into English. He was born in Gloucestershire (where his family seems to have used the name of Hutchins or Hychins, as well as that of Tyndale, so that he is himself sometimes described by both names); and he became a member of Magdalen Hall (a dependency of Magdalen College) at Oxford, where he definitely associated himself with the Protestant party and became known as one of their leaders. He took his degree as B.A. in 1512, as M.A. in 1515, and at some uncertain date, he is said (by Foxe) to have gone to Cambridge. If this was between 1511 and 1515, he would have found Erasmus there; but in that case it could have been only an interlude in the middle of his Oxford course, and perhaps it is more probable that his visit belongs to some part of the years 1515 to 1520, as to which there is no definite information. About 1520 he became resident tutor in the house of Sir John Walsh, at Little Sodbury in Gloucestershire, to which period belongs his famous saying, in controversy with an opponent: "If God spare my life, ere many years I will cause a boy that driveth the plow shall know more of the Scriptures than thou dost." With this object, he came up to London in 1523 and sought a place in the service of Tunstall, bishop of London, a scholar and patron of scholars, of whom Erasmus had spoken favorably, but here he received no encouragement. He was, however, taken in by Alderman Humphrey Monmouth, in whose house he lived as chaplain and studied for six months; at the end of which time he was forced to the conclusion "not only that there was no room in my Lord of London's palace to translate the New Testament, but also that there was no place to do it in all England."

About May 1524, therefore, Tyndale left England and settled in the free city of Hamburg, and in the course of the next 12 months, the first stage of his great work was completed. Whether during this time he visited Luther at Wittenberg is quite uncertain; what is certain, and more important, is that he was acquainted with Luther's writings. In 1525, the translation of the New Testament being finished, he went to Cologne to have it printed at the press of Peter Quentel. Three thousand copies of the first ten sheets of it, in quarto, had been printed off when rumors of the work came to the ears of John Cochlaeus, a bitter enemy of the

Reformation. To obtain information he approached the printers (who were also engaged upon work for him), and having loosened their tongues with wine he learned the full details of Tyndale's enterprise and sent warning forthwith to England. Meanwhile, Tyndale escaped with the printed sheets to Worms, in the Lutheran disposition of which place he was secure from interference, and proceeded with his work at the press of Peter Schoeffer. Since, however, a description of the Cologne edition had been sent to England, a change was made in the format. The text was set up again in octavo, and without the marginal notes of the quarto edition; and in this form, the first printed English New Testament was given to the world early in 1526. About the same time an edition in small quarto, with marginal notes, was also issued, and it is probable (though full proof is wanting) that this was the completion of the interrupted Cologne edition. Three thousand copies of each edition were struck off; but so active were the enemies of the Reformation in their destruction, that they have nearly disappeared off the face of the earth. One copy of the octavo edition, complete but for the loss of its title-page, is at the Baptist College at Bristol, whither it found its way from the Harley Library, to which it once belonged; and an imperfect copy is in the library of St. Paul's Cathedral. Of the quarto, all that survives is a fragment consisting of eight sheets (Mat 1:1–22:12) in the Grenville Library in the British Museum.

The hostility of the authorities in church and state in England was indeed undisguised. Sir Thomas More attacked the translation as false and heretical, and as disregarding ecclesiastical terminology. Wolsey and the bishops, with Henry's assent, decreed that it should be burnt; and burnt it was at Paul's Cross, after a sermon from Bishop Tunstall. Nevertheless, fresh supplies continued to pour into England, the money expended in buying up copies for destruction serving to pay for the production of fresh editions. Six editions are said to have been issued between 1526 and 1530; and the zeal of the authorities for its destruction was fairly matched by the zeal of the reforming party for its circulation. I was, in fact, evident that the appetite for an English Bible, once fairly excited, could not be wholly balked. In 1530 an assembly convoked by Archbishop Warham, while maintaining the previous condemnation of Tyndale, and asserting that it was not expedient at that time to divulge the Scripture in the English tongue, announced that the king would have the New Testament faithfully translated by learned men, and published "as soon as he might see their manners and behavior meet, apt, and convenient to receive the same."

Tyndale's first New Testament was epoch-making in many ways. It was the first English printed New Testament; it laid the foundations, and much more than the foundations, of the Authorized Version of 1611; it set on foot the movement which went forward without a break until it culminated in the production of that Authorized Version, and it was the first English Bible that was translated directly from the original language. All the English manuscript Bibles were translations from the Vulgate; but Tyndale's New Testament was taken from the Greek, which he knew from the editions by Erasmus, published in 1516, 1519, and 1522. As subsidiary aids he employed the Latin version attached by Erasmus to his Greek text, Luther's German translation of 1522, and the Vulgate; but it has been made abundantly clear that he exercised independent judgment in the use of these materials, and was by no means a slavish copier of Luther. In the marginal notes attached to the quarto edition his debt to Luther was greater; for (so far as can be gathered from the extant fragment) more than half the notes were taken directly from the German Bible, the rest being independent. It is in this connection with Luther, rather than in anything to be found in the work itself, that the secret of the official hostility to Tyndale's version is to be found. That the translation itself was not seriously to blame is shown by the extent to which it was incorporated in the Authorized Version, though no doubt to persons who knew the Scriptures only in the Latin Vulgate its divergence from accuracy may have appeared greater than was, in fact, the case. The octavo edition had no extraneous matter except a short preface, and therefore could not be obnoxious on controversial grounds, and the comments in the quarto edition are generally exegetical, and not polemical. Still, there could be no doubt that they were the work of an adherent of the Reformation, and as such the whole translation fell under the ban of the opponents of the Reformation.

Tyndale's work did not cease with the production of his New Testament. Early in 1530 a translation of the Pentateuch was printed for him by Hans Luft, at Marburg in Hesse. The colophon to Genesis is dated Jan. 17, 1530. In England, where the year began on March 25, this would have meant 1531 according to our modern reckoning; but in Germany the year generally began on Jan. 1, or at Christmas. The only perfect copy of this edition is in the British Museum. The different books must have been set up separately, since Genesis and Numbers are printed in black letter, Exodus, Leviticus and Deuteronomy in roman; but there is no evidence that they were issued separately. The translation was made (for the first time) from the Hebrew, with which language there is express evidence that Tyndale was acquainted. The book was provided with a prologue and with marginal notes, the latter being often controversial. In 1531 he published a translation of the book of Jonah, of which a single copy (now in the British Museum) came to light in 1861. After this he seems to have reverted to the New Testament, of which he issued a revised edition in 1534. The immediate occasion of this was the appearance of an unauthorized revision of the translation of 1525, by one George Joye, in which many alterations were made of which Tyndale disapproved. Tyndale's new edition was printed by Martin Empereur of Antwerp, and published on November 1534. One copy of it was printed on vellum, illuminated, and presented to Anne Boleyn, who had shown favor to one of the agents employed in distributing Tyndale's earlier work. It bears her name on the fore-edge, and is now in the British Museum. The volume is a small octavo, and embodies a careful revision of his previous work. Since it was intended for liturgical use, the church lections were marked in it, and in an appendix were added, "The Epistles taken out of the Old Testament, which are read in the church after the use of Salisbury upon certain days of the year." These consist of 42 short passages from the Old Testament (8 being taken from the Apocrypha) and constitute an addition to Tyndale's work as a translator of the Old Testament. The text of the New Testament is accompanied throughout by marginal notes, differing (as far as we are in a position to compare them) from those in the quarto of 1525, and very rarely polemical. Nearly all the books are preceded by prologues, which are for the most part derived from Luther (except that to Hebrews, in which Tyndale expressly combats Luther's rejection of its Apostolic authority).

The edition of 1534 did not finally satisfy Tyndale, and in the following year he put forth another edition "yet once again corrected." (The volume bears two dates, 1535 and 1534, but the former, which stands on the first title-page, must be taken to be that of the completion of the work.) It bears the monogram of the publisher, Godfried van der Haghen, and is sometimes known as the GH edition. It has no marginal notes. Another edition, which is stated on its title-page to have been finished in 1535, contains practically the same text, but is notable for its spelling, which appears to be due to a Flemish compositor, working by ear and not by sight. These editions of 1535, which embody several small changes from the text of 1534, represent Tyndale's work in its final form. Several editions were issued in 1536, but Tyndale was not then in a position to supervise them. In May 1535, through the treachery of one Phillips, he was siezed by some officers of the emperor and carried off from Antwerp (where he had lived for a year past) to the castle of Vilvorde. After some months' imprisonment he was brought to trial, condemned, and finally strangled and burnt at the stake on October 6, 1536, crying "with a fervent, great, and a loud voice, 'Lord, open the King of England's eyes.'"

CHAPTER 6 The Betrayal and Death of the Translator William Tyndale

Edward D. Andrews

We have a young man, who is a has been on the run from the Catholic church for many years, all the while working as a printer and a translator of the English Bible. Many times, there was a pounding at the door, only to find that this translator and his apprentice has left moments earlier. The Catholic Church viewed the Bible in the language of the common people as illegal literature, because the people were too illiterate to understand the Word of God. The Bible had been locked up in the dead language of Latin for almost a thousand years. Who was the translator? He was William Tyndale, i.e., "God's Outlaw," who had been pursued by the false friend of the Catholic Church, as though he were the worst criminal on the planet in the early 16th-century. While King James is credited with the most popular Bible that has ever been published, it was actually William Tyndale who should be credited, because the 1611 King James Version was 97 percent Tyndale's English translation. The Word of God has had many enemies since the first book, Genesis, was published, some 3,500 years ago.

The clergy were extremely bitterly opposed to Tyndale's translation. Why? The Latin *Vulgate* had a tendency of veiling the sacred text for 500 years, while Tyndale's translation from the original Greek conveyed the Bible's message in clear language to the people of England for the first time. For instance, Tyndale chose to translate the Greek word *agape* as "love" instead of "charity" in 1 Corinthians chapter 13. He rendered the Greek word ecclesia as "congregation" as opposed to "church" so as to emphasize worshipers, rather than church buildings. This took the power back from the church and gave it to the people. The last in a series of unpleasant events that finally made the Catholic Church feel that they could not continue to accept William Tyndale's translation not his existence was when he replaced "priest" with "elder" and used "repent" rather than "do penance." Tyndale in so doing stripped the clergy of their assumed priestly powers. David Daniell says in this regard: "Catholic revisionists are not there; **Purgatory is not there; there is no aural confession and penance. Two supports of the Church's wealth and power collapsed.** Instead, there was simply individual faith in Christ as Saviour, found in Scripture." (*William Tyndale—A Biography*, 58) That was the difficult that Tyndale's translation place on the Catholic Church, and modern-day scholarship fully endorses the correctness of his word choices.

Between 1526 and 1528, Tyndale moved to Antwerp. It was here that he felt a little safe among the English merchants. There he wrote *The Parable of the Wicked Mammon, The Obedience of a Christian Man*, and *The Practice of Prelates.* Tyndale never abandoned his translation work. Another step toward the accuracy of Tyndale's translation was the fact that he was the first to use God's personal name, Jehovah, in an English translation of the Hebrew Old Testament Scriptures. The divine name appears over 20 times. It would also be used 4 times in the 1611 King James Version as well.

Eventually, the Englishman Henry Phillips cunningly inveigled himself into Tyndale's confidences. "Henry Phillips was the third and last son in the family ... Phillips threw himself into the company of the English merchants, and by his silver tongue and golden hand won the confidence of all except Thomas Poyntz, the man who gave Tyndale safe lodging in Antwerp. It was not long before Tyndale, who was frequently invited to dine with the merchants, found himself in the same company, and Henry Phillips had come face to face with his prey. Unsuspecting, the reformer felt attracted to the easy manner and eloquent speech of the young student lawyer, and before long he invited him to the Poyntzes' home. There he dined, admired Tyndale's small library, warmly commended his labors, and talked easily of the affairs in England and the need for reform. He even stayed overnight. Thomas Poyntz had misgivings about the relative stranger, but when Tyndale assured him of the man's Lutheran sympathies, he put his doubts aside. This was the greatest mistake Tyndale ever made."[13] As a result, in 1535, Tyndale was betrayed and taken to Vilvorde Castle, which was six miles north of Brussels. There he was imprisoned for sixteen months.

> The castle of Vilvoorde had been erected in 1374 by one of the dukes of Brabant, and since it was modeled upon the infamous Bastille, built in Paris at about the same time, its moat, seven towers, three drawbridges and massive walls made it an impregnable prison. The castle was used as the state prison for the Low Countries, and Tyndale was thrown into one of the foul—smelling, damp dungeons with nothing for company but the lapping moat, the squabbling moorhens outside, and the dripping walls and scurrying rats inside. Here, in his solitary darkness, Tyndale waited for the end.[14]

---

[13] Retrieved Monday, August 5, 2019
https://christianhistoryinstitute.org/magazine/article/tyndales-betrayal-and-death
[14] IBID.

William Tyndale like others before him and others who would come after him would give his life, so that the people of England could have an accurate Bible translation. He paid the ultimate price, but he also gave us the priceless gift! Dr. Leland Ryken of Wheaton College helps us better appreciate just what received from Tyndale

This essay is a historical study. That may seem anomalous in a journal devoted to current translation issues and practices, so a word of explanation is in order. One of the functions of inquiring into the history of English Bible translation is that it can clarify the essential principles of Bible translation. When the issues are distanced from us in time, we can see some things more clearly because they are unclouded by contemporary crosswinds.

More important than the clarifying power of distance, though, is the authority that attaches to historical precedents. This authority may or not be completely valid, but it is a fact that in the current debate between rival translation philosophies an appeal to historical precedents is considered important. Both literal translators and dynamic equivalent and colloquial translators probe the past to find examples of their own preferred style of translation.

The current debate about William Tyndale

It is obvious that we live in a day of debunking. On the Bible translation scene, advocates of colloquial English Bible translations regularly and rigorously debunk the King James Version. In turn, it has become common for these debunkers to attempt to drive a wedge between the King James Version and William Tyndale's translation work nearly a century earlier.

More specifically, the claim is made that the King James translators spoiled Tyndale by refining his style. Eugene Peterson, the author of The Message, has, of course, led the charge, but he is not alone. Predictably, the claim is made that Tyndale produced a colloquial translation while the King James translation is elegant. Peterson claims that the King James translators "desecrated language upwards" [Eat This Book (Grand Rapids: Eerdmans, 2006), 162].

The most famous statement that Tyndale made about Bible translation, next to his dying prayer that God would open the king of England's eyes, is a comment that he made about wanting the plowboy to know the Bible better than the Catholic priests. I will quote the statement shortly and then analyze it, but as a lead-in to that, I need to note that translators in what I call the "modernizing" camp claim that Tyndale in a single utterance endorsed (1) a colloquial style for an English Bible, (2) an uneducated reader as the assumed audience for an English Bible, and (3) a dynamic equivalent philosophy of translation (buttressed, of course, by a few famous examples from Tyndale's actual translation). My thesis in this article is that Tyndale's plowboy statement has been extravagantly misinterpreted and that none of the three conclusions I listed in the previous sentence is warranted.

Exactly what did Tyndale say?

Tyndale's plowboy statement is recounted in John Foxe's Book of Martyrs. The context of the statement itself disproves the use to which modernizing translators put it. Tyndale had uttered the statement before he had even begun his work of translating the Bible. The occasion of the statement was not Bible translation per se. Instead, the statement occurred as part of the debate about whether the pope or the Bible is the ultimate authority for religious belief and practice.

Upon graduating from Oxford University, Tyndale returned to his native Gloucestershire and assumed the position as a schoolmaster in the Catholic household of Sir John Walsh. Tyndale was an early Reformer whose views brought him into heated debates with the local clergy. Tyndale was appalled at the ignorance of the Catholic clergy. Additionally, he was convinced of the Protestant doctrine of sola scriptura on the question of religious authority. I propose that these two things, the biblical ignorance of the clergy and the question of biblical authority, are the context for Tyndale's statement about the plowboy.

We can hear these two themes of biblical ignorance among the clergy and the authority of Bible in the statement that I now quote:

> There dwelt not far off a certain doctor, that he been chancellor to a bishop, who had been of old, familiar acquaintance with Master Tyndale, and favored him well; unto whom Master Tyndale went and opened his mind upon divers questions of the Scripture: for to him he durst be bold to disclose his heart. Unto whom the doctor said, "Do you not know that the pope is very Antichrist, whom the Scripture speaketh of? But beware what you say; for if you shall be perceived to be of that opinion, it will cost you your life." Not long after, Master Tyndale happened to be in the company of a certain divine, recounted for a learned man, and, in communing and disputing with him, he drove him to that

issue, that the said great doctor burst out into these blasphemous words, "We were better to be without God's laws than the pope's." Master Tyndale, hearing this, full of godly zeal, and not bearing that blasphemous saying, replied, "I defy the pope, and all his laws;" and added, "If God spared him life, ere many years he would cause a boy that driveth the plough to know more of the Scripture than he did." The grudge of the priests increasing still more and more against Tyndale, they never ceased barking and rating at him, and laid many things sorely to his charge, saying that he was a heretic.

We should note first what is not going on here. The statement about the plowboy is not a comment about Tyndale's preferred style for an English Bible. It is not a designation of teenage farm boys as a target audience for a niche Bible. In fact, the account does not even mention translation of the Bible into English. Foxe's account makes it clear that the subject of debate at this early stage in Tyndale's career was the question of papal authority vs. scriptural authority. When the priest asserted a strong view of papal authority and denigrated the authority of the Bible, Tyndale responded by making an implied case for the Bible as the authority for Christian belief and conduct. We should not overlook Foxe's follow-up comment about "the grudge of the priests." The plowboy statement is part of a debate with Catholic priests over papal authority, not on the style of an English Bible.

Therefore, what did Tyndale mean in his famous plowboy statement? First, he implicitly asserted the right of the laity to the Bible. The plowboy is a representative of the whole of English society. Tyndale's statement is not a comment about English style but about how widely Tyndale wanted the English Bible to be disseminated in English society. Even the humble working class should have access to the Bible.

Secondly, Tyndale was making a statement about how much of the Bible he wanted the laity to know. His statement, to quote again, is "that he would cause a boy that driveth the plough to know more of the Scripture than [the priest] did." The typical priest knew the snatches of Scripture that were embedded in the liturgy, the mass, and choral music, and he would have known it in Latin.

What I most want to challenge is the view that Tyndale was an ally of what I call modernizing and colloquializing English Bibles that have proliferated since the middle of the twentieth century. Whatever we conclude about Tyndale's preferred style in English translation is something we need to deduce from his actual translation, not from his statement about the plowboy.

Conclusion

Tyndale's plowboy statement is a virtual Rorschach inkblot [interpretation] in which modern translators sees what they themselves believe about English Bible translation. In turn, Tyndale is such a towering figure that if one can claim him for one's side in the translation wars, it is, in fact, a victory. I submit that Tyndale's plowboy statement should not be allowed to lend any support whatever to dynamic equivalent and colloquial translations. Exactly where Tyndale stood on questions of essentially literal vs. dynamic equivalence and dignified vs. colloquial style needs to rest on his actual translation of the Bible.

By 1538, King Henry VIII for whatever reason came to order that Bibles be placed in every church in England. While William Tyndale was not given the credit, the translation that was decided upon was essentially his Bible. In this way, Tyndale's translation work was so well-known and cherished that it "determined the fundamental character of most of the subsequent versions" in English. (The Cambridge History of the Bible) As much as 90 percent of the Tyndale translation was transferred directly into the 1611 King James Bible. And so, it was that William Tyndale was martyred (gave his life) for the honor of giving a Bible that could easily be understood to the people of England. What a price he had paid, however; it was a priceless gift! Tyndale with his skills and gift of language had done his work well; he had made the Word of God known to the common people. Tyndale and others before and after him had worked with the shadow of death towering over their heads. However, by delivering the Bible to many people in their native tongue, they opened up before them the possibility, not of death, but of life eternal. As Jesus Christ said in the Tyndale Bible, "This is lyfe eternall that they myght knowe the that only very God and whom thou hast sent Iesus Christ." (John 17:3) May we, therefore, know the value of what we can now hold in our hands and may we diligently study God's Word.

CHAPTER 7 Miles Coverdale's Bible (1535)

Frederic G. Kenyon

Tyndale never had the satisfaction of completing his gift of an English Bible to his country; but during his imprisonment, he may have learned that a complete translation, based largely upon his own, had actually been produced. The credit for this achievement, the first complete printed English Bible, is due to Miles Coverdale (1488-1569), afterward bishop of Exeter (1551-1553). The details of its production are obscure. Coverdale met Tyndale abroad in 1529 and is said to have assisted him in the translation of the Pentateuch. His own work was done under the patronage of Cromwell, who was anxious for the publication of an English Bible; and it was no doubt forwarded by the action of Convocation, which, under Cranmer's leading, had petitioned in 1534 for the undertaking of such a work. It was probably printed by Froschover at Zurich, but this has never been absolutely demonstrated. It was published at the end of 1535, with a dedication to Henry VIII. By this time the conditions were more favorable to a Protestant Bible than they had been in 1525. Henry had finally broken with the Pope and had committed himself to the principle of an English Bible. Coverdale's work was accordingly tolerated by authority, and when the second edition of it appeared in 1537 (printed by an English printer, Nycolson of Southwark), it bore on its title-page the words, "Set forth with the Kinng's most gracious license." In thus licensing Coverdale's translation, Henry probably did not know how far he was sanctioning the work of Tyndale, which he had previously condemned. In the New Testament, in particular, Tyndale's version is the basis of Coverdale's, and to a somewhat less extent this is also the case in the Pentateuch and Jonah; but Coverdale revised the work of his predecessor with the help of the Zurich German Bible of Zwingli and others (1524-1529), a Latin version by Pagninus, the Vulgate, and Luther. In his preface, he explicitly disclaims originality as a translator, and there is no sign that he made any noticeable use of the Greek and Hebrew; but he used the available Latin, German, and English versions with judgment. In the parts of the Old Testament which Tyndale had not published he appears to have translated mainly from the Zurich Bible. [Coverdale's Bible of 1535 was reprinted by Bagster, 1838.]

In one respect Coverdale's Bible was epoch-making, namely, in the arrangement of the books of the Old Testament. In the Vulgate, as is well known, the books which are now classed as Apocrypha are intermingled with the other books of the Old Testament. This was also the case with the

Septuagint, and in general, it may be said that the Christian church had adopted this view of the canon. It is true that many of the greatest Christian Fathers had protested against it, and had preferred the Hebrew canon, which rejects these books. The canon of Athanasius places the Apocrypha in a class apart; the Syrian Bible omitted them; Eusebius and Gregory Nazianzen appear to have held similar views, and Jerome refused to translate them for his Latin Bible. Nevertheless the church at large, both East and West, retained them in their Bibles, and the provincial Council of Carthage (A.D. 397), under the influence of Augustine, expressly included them in the canon. In spite of Jerome, the Vulgate, as it circulated in Western Europe, regularly included the disputed books; and Wyclif's Bible, being a translation from the Vulgate, naturally has them too. On the other hand, Luther, though recognizing these books as profitable and good for reading, placed them in a class apart, as "Apocrypha," and in the same way he segregated Hebrews, James, Jude, and the Apocalypse at the end of the New Testament, as of less value and authority than the rest. This arrangement appears in the table of contents of Tyndale's New Testament in 1525 and was adopted by Coverdale, Matthew, and Taverner. It is to Tyndale's example, no doubt, that the action of Coverdale is due. His Bible is divided into six parts -- (1) Pentateuch; (2) Joshua -- Esther; (3) Job -- "Solomon's Balettes" (i.e. Canticles); (4) Prophets; (5) "Apocrypha, the books and treatises which among the fathers of old are not reckoned to be of like authority with the other books of the Bible, neither are they found in the canon of the Hebrew"; (6) the New Testament. This represents the view generally taken by the Reformers, both in Germany and in England, and so far as concerns the English Bible, Coverdale's example was decisive. On the other hand, the Roman Church, at the Council of Trent (1546), adopted by a majority the opinion that all the books of the larger canon should be received as of equal authority, and for the first time made this a dogma of the Church, enforced by an anathema. In 1538, Coverdale published a New Testament with Latin (Vulgate) and English in parallel columns, revising his English to bring it into conformity with the Latin; but this (which went through three editions with various changes) may be passed over, as it had no influence on the general history of the English Bible.

CHAPTER 8 Matthew's Bible (1537) and Taverner's Bible (1539)

Frederic G. Kenyon

In the same year as the second edition of Coverdale's Bible, another English Bible appeared, which likewise bore upon its title-page the statement that it was "set forth with the king's most gracious license." It was completed not later than August 4, 1537, on which day Cranmer sent a copy of it to Cromwell, commending the translation, and begging Cromwell to obtain for it the king's license; in which, as the title-page prominently shows, he was successful. The origin of this version is slightly obscure and certainly was not realized by Henry when he sanctioned it. The Pentateuch and New Testament are taken directly from Tyndale with little variation (the latter from the final "GH" revision of 1535). The books of the Old Testament from Ezra to Malachi (including Jonah) are taken from Coverdale, as also is the Apocrypha. But the historical books of the Old Testament (Joshua through 2 Chronicles) are a new translation, as to the origin of which no statement is made. It is, however, reasonably certain, from a combination of evidence, that it was Tyndale's (see Westcott, 3rd ed., pp. 169-179). The style agrees with that of Tyndale's other work; the passages which Tyndale published as "Epistles" from the Old Testament in his New Testament of 1534 agree in the main with the present version in these books, but not in those taken from Coverdale; and it is expressly stated in Hall's *Chronicle* (completed and published by Grafton, one of the publishers of Matthew's Bible) that Tyndale, in addition to the New Testament, translated also "the v bookes of Moses, Josua, Judicum, Ruth, the bookes of the Kynges and the bookes of Paralipomenon [Chronicles], Nehemias or the first of Esdras, the prophet Jonas, and no more of ye holy scripture." If we suppose the version of Ezra-Nehemiah to have been incomplete, or for some reason, unavailable, this statement harmonizes perfectly with the data of the problem. Tyndale may have executed the translation during his imprisonment, at which time we know that he applied for the use of his Hebrew books. The book was printed abroad, at the expense of R. Grafton and E. Whitchurch, two citizens of London, who issued it in London. On the title-page is the statement that the translator was Thomas Matthew, and the same name stands at the foot of the dedication to Henry VIII. Nothing is known of any such person, but tradition identifies him with **John Rogers** (who in the register of his arrest in 1555 is described as "John Rogers *alias* Matthew"), a friend and companion of Tyndale. It is therefore generally believed that this Bible is due to the editorial work of John Rogers, who had come into possession of Tyndale's unpublished translation of the historical books of the Old Testament and published them with the rest of his friend's work, completing the Bible with the help of Coverdale. It may be added that the initials I.R. (Ioannes Rogers), W.T. (Tyndale), R.G. and E.W. (Grafton and Whitchurch), and H.R. (unidentified, Henricus Rex?) are printed in large letters on various blank spaces throughout the Old Testament. The arrangement of the book is in four sections: (1) Genesis -- Canticles, (2) Prophets, (3) Apocrypha (including for the first time the Prayer of Manasses, translated from the French of Olivetan), (4) New Testament. There are copious annotations, of a decidedly Protestant tendency, and Tyndale's outspoken Prologue to the Romans is included in it. The whole work, therefore, was eminently calculated to extend the impulse given by Tyndale, and to perpetuate his work.

Taverner's Bible (1539)

Matthew's Bible formed the basis for yet another version, which deserves brief mention, though it had no influence on the general development of the English Bible. Richard Taverner, formerly a student of Cardinal College [Christ Church], Oxford, was invited by some London printers ("John Byddell for Thomas Barthlet") to prepare at short notice a revision of the existing Bible. In the Old Testament, his alterations are verbal and aim at the improvement of the style of the translation; in the New Testament, being a good Greek scholar, he was able to revise it with reference to the original Greek. The New Testament was issued separately in two editions in the same year (1539) as the complete Bible, but the success of the official version next to be mentioned [the Great Bible] speedily extinguished such a personal venture as this. Taverner's Bible is sometimes said to have been the first English Bible completely printed in England, but this honor appears to belong instead to Coverdale's second edition.

CHAPTER 9 The Great Bible (1539-1541)

Frederic G. Kenyon

The fact that Taverner was invited to revise Matthew's Bible almost immediately after its publication shows that it was not universally regarded as successful, but there were, in addition, other reasons why those who had promoted the circulation and authorization of Matthew's Bible should be anxious to see it superseded. As stated above, it was highly controversial in character and bore plentiful evidence of its origin from Tyndale. Cromwell and Cranmer had, no doubt, been careful not to call Henry's attention to these circumstances, but they might at any time be brought to his notice when their own position would become highly precarious. It is, indeed, strange that they ever embarked on so risky an enterprise. However that maybe, they lost little time in inviting Coverdale to undertake a complete revision of the whole, which was ready for the press early in 1538. The printing was begun by Regnault of Paris, where more beautiful typography was possible than in England. In spite, however, of the assent of the French king having been obtained, the Inquisition intervened, stopped the printing, and seized the sheets. Some of the sheets, however, had previously been got away to England; others were re-purchased from a tradesman to whom they had been sold; and ultimately, under Cromwell's direction, printers and presses were transported from Paris to London, and the work completed thereby Grafton and Whitchurch, whose imprint stands on the magnificent title-page (traditionally ascribed to Holbein) depicting the dissemination of the Scriptures from the hands of Henry, through the instrumentality of Cromwell and Cranmer, to the general mass of the loyal and rejoicing populace. [A special copy on vellum, with illuminations, was prepared for Cromwell himself, and is now in the library of St. John's College, Cambridge.]

The first edition of the Great Bible appeared in April 1539, and an injunction was issued by Cromwell that a copy of it should be set up in every parish church. It was consequently the first (and only) English Bible formally authorized for public use, and contemporary evidence proves that it was welcomed and read with avidity. No doubt, as at an earlier day (Philippians 2:15), some read the gospel "of envy and strife, and some also of goodwill"; but in one way or another, for edification or for controversy, the reading of the Bible took a firm hold on the people of England, a hold which has never since been relaxed, and which had much to do with the stable foundation of the Protestant church in this country. Nor was the translation, though still falling short of the perfection reached three-quarters of a century later, unworthy of its position. It had many positive merits and marked a distinct advance upon all its predecessors. Coverdale, though without the force and originality, or even the scholarship, of Tyndale, had some of the more valuable gifts of a translator, and was well qualified to make the best use of the labors of his predecessors. He had scholarship enough to choose and follow the best authorities, he had a delightful gift of smooth and effective phraseology, and his whole heart was in his work. As the basis of his revision he had Tyndale's work and his own previous version; and these he revised with reference to the Hebrew, Greek, and Latin, with special assistance in the Old Testament from the Latin translation by Sebastian Münster published in 1534-35 (a work decidedly superior to the Zurich Bible, which had been his principal guide in 1534), while in the New Testament he made considerable use of Erasmus.

With regard to the use of ecclesiastical terms, he followed his own previous example, against Tyndale, in retaining the familiar Latin phrases; and he introduced a considerable number of words and sentences from the Vulgate, which do not appear in the Hebrew or Greek. The text is divided into five sections — (1) Pentateuch, (2) Joshua — Job, (3) Psalms — Malachi, (4) Apocrypha, here entitled "Hagiographa," though quite different from the books to which that term is applied in the Hebrew Bible, (5) New Testament, in which the traditional order of the books is restored in place of Luther's. Coverdale intended to add a commentary at the end, and with this view inserted various marks in the margins, the purpose of which he explains in the Prologue; but he was unable to obtain the sanction of the Privy Council for these, and after standing in the margin for three editions the sign-post marks were withdrawn.

The first edition was exhausted within twelve months, and in April 1540 a second edition appeared, this time with a prologue by Cranmer (from which fact the Great Bible is sometimes known as Cranmer's Bible, though he had no part in the translation). Two more editions followed in July and November, the latter (Cromwell having now been overthrown and executed) appearing under the nominal patronage of bishops Tunstall and Heath. In 1541 three editions were issued. None of these editions was a simple reprint. The Prophets, in particular, were carefully revised with the help of Münster for the second edition. The fourth edition (November 1540) and its successors revert in part to the first. These seven editions spread the knowledge of the Bible in a sound, though not perfect, version broadcast through the land, and one portion of it has never lost its place in our liturgy. In the first Prayer Book of Edward VI, the Psalter (like the other Scripture passages) was taken from the Great Bible. In 1662, when the other passages were taken from the version of 1611, a special exception was made of the Psalter, on account of the familiarity which it had achieved, and consequently Coverdale's version has held its place in the Book of Common Prayer to this day, and it is in his words that the Psalms have become the familiar household treasures of the English people.

With the appearance of the Great Bible comes the first pause in the rapid sequence of vernacular versions set on foot by Tyndale. The English Bible was now fully authorized and accessible to every Englishman in his parish church; and the translation, both in style and in scholarship, was fairly abreast of the attainments and requirements of the age. We hear no more, therefore, at present of further revisions of it. Another circumstance that may have contributed to the same result was the reaction of Henry in his later years against Protestantism. There was talk in Convocation about a translation to be made by the bishops, which anticipated the plan of the Bible of 1568 [the Bishops' Bible]; and Cranmer prompted Henry to transfer the work to the universities, which anticipated a vital part of the plan of the Bible of 1611; but nothing came of either project. The only practical steps taken were in the direction of the destruction of the earlier versions. In 1543 a proclamation was issued against Tyndale's versions, and requiring the obliteration of all notes; in 1546 Coverdale's New Testament was likewise prohibited. The anti-Protestant reaction, however, was soon terminated by Henry's death (January 1547); and during the reign of Edward VI, though no new translation (except a small part of the Gospels by Sir J. Cheke) was attempted, many new editions of Tyndale, Coverdale, Matthew, and the Great Bible issued from the press. The accession of Mary naturally put a stop to the printing and circulation of vernacular Bibles in England; and, during the attempt to put the clock back by force, Rogers and Cranmer followed Tyndale to the stake, while Coverdale was imprisoned, but was released, and took refuge at Geneva.

CHAPTER 11 The Geneva Bible (1557-1560)

Frederic G. Kenyon

Geneva was the place at which the next link in the chain was to be forged. Already famous, through the work of Beza, as a center of Biblical scholarship, it became the rallying place of the more advanced members of the Protestant party in exile, and under the strong rule of Calvin, it was identified with Puritanism in its most rigid form. Puritanism, in fact, was here consolidated into a living and active principle and demonstrated its strength as a motive power in the religious and social life of Europe. It was by a relative of Calvin, and under his own patronage, that the work of improving the English translation of the Bible was once more taken in hand. This was William Whittingham, a Fellow of All Souls' College, Oxford, and subsequently dean of Durham, who in 1557 published the New Testament at Geneva in a small octavo volume, the handiest form in which the English Scriptures had yet been given to the world. In two other respects also this marked an epoch in the history of the English Bible. It was the first version to be printed in roman type and the first in which the division of the text into numbered verses (originally made by Robert Stephanus for his Greaco-Latin Bible of 1551) was introduced. A preface was contributed by Calvin himself. The translator claims to have made constant use of the original Greek and of translations in other tongues, and he added a full marginal commentary. If the matter had ended there, as the work of a single scholar on one part of the Bible, it would probably have left little mark; but it was at once made the basis of a revised version of both Testaments by a group of Puritan scholars. The details of the work are not recorded, but the principal workers, apart from Whittingham himself, appear to have been Thomas Sampson, formerly dean of Chichester, and afterward dean of Christ Church, and A. Gilby, of Christ's College, Cambridge. A version of the Psalter was issued in 1559 [the only two extant copies of it belong to the Earl of Ellesmere and Mr. Aldis Wright], and in 1560 the complete Bible was given to the world, with the imprint of Rowland Hall, at Geneva. The Psalter in this was the same as that of 1559, but the New Testament had been largely revised since 1557. The book was a moderate-sized quarto, and contained a dedication to Elizabeth, an address to the brethren at home, the books of the Old Testament (including Apocrypha) and New Testament in the same order as in the Great Bible and our modern Bibles, copious marginal notes (those to the New Testament taken from Whittingham with some additions), and an apparatus of maps and woodcuts. In type and verse-division it followed the example of Whittingham's New Testament.

The Genevan revisers took the Great Bible as their basis in the Old Testament and Matthew's Bible (i.e. Tyndale) in the New Testament. For the former, they had the assistance of the Latin Bible of Leo Juda (1544), in addition to Pagninus (1527), and they were in consultation with the scholars (including Calvin and Beza) who were then engaged at Geneva in a similar work of revision of the French Bible. In the New Testament, their principal guide was Beza, whose reputation stood highest among all the Biblical scholars of the age. The result was a version that completely distanced its predecessors in scholarship, while in style and vocabulary it worthily carried on the great tradition established by Tyndale. Its success was as decisive as it was well deserved, and in one respect it met a want which none of its predecessors (except perhaps Tyndale's) had attempted to meet. Coverdale's, Matthew's, and the Great Bible were all large folios, suitable for use in church, but unsuited both in size and in price for private possession and domestic study. The Geneva Bible, on the contrary, was moderate in both respects and achieved instant and long-enduring popularity as the Bible for personal use. For a full century, it continued to be the Bible of the people, and it was upon this version, and not upon that of King James, that the Bible knowledge of the Puritans of the Civil War was built up. Its notes furnished them with a full commentary on the sacred text, predominantly horatory or monitory in character, but Calvinistic in general tone, and occasionally definitely polemical. Over 160 editions of it are said to have been issued, but the only one which requires separate notice is a revision of the New Testament by Laurence Thomson in 1576, which carried still further the principle of deference to Beza; this revised New Testament was successful, and was frequently bound up with the Genevan Old Testament in place of the edition of 1560.

CHAPTER 12 The Bishops' Bible (1568)

Frederic G. Kenyon

Meanwhile, there was one quarter in which the Geneva Bible could hardly be expected to find favor, namely, among the leaders of the Church of England. Elizabeth herself was not too well disposed towards the Puritans, and the bishops, in general, belonged to the less extreme party in the church. On the other hand, the superiority of the Genevan to the Great Bible could not be contested. Under these circumstances, the old project of a translation to be produced by the bishops was revived. The archbishop of Canterbury, Matthew Parker, was himself a scholar and took up the task with interest. The basis of the new version was to be the authorized Great Bible. Portions of the text were assigned to various revisers, the majority of whom were bishops. The archbishop exercised general supervision over the work, but there does not appear to have been any organized system of collaboration or revision, and the results were naturally unequal. In the Old Testament, the alterations were mainly verbal [stylistic], and do not show much originality or genius. In the New Testament, the scholarship shown is on a much higher level, and there is much more independence in style and judgment. In both, use is made of the Geneva Bible, as well as of other versions. The volume was equipped with notes, shorter than those of the Geneva Bible, and generally exegetical. It appeared in 1568, from the press of R. Jugge, in a large folio volume, slightly exceeding even the dimensions of the Great Bible. Parker applied through Cecil for the royal sanction, but it does not appear that he ever obtained it; but Convocation in 1571 required a copy to be kept in every archbishop's and bishop's house and in every cathedral, and, as far as could conveniently be done, in all churches. The Bishops' Bible, in fact, superseded the Great Bible as the official version, and its predecessor ceased henceforth to be reprinted; but it never attained the popularity and influence of the Geneva Bible. A second edition was issued in 1569, in which a considerable number of alterations were made, partly, it appears, as the result of the criticisms of Giles Laurence, professor of Greek at Oxford. In 1572 a third edition appeared, of importance chiefly in the New Testament, and in some cases reverting to the first edition of 1568. In this form, the Bishops' Bible continued in official use until its supersession by the version of 1611, of which it formed the immediate basis.

The Bishop's Bible succeeded the Great Bible of 1539, the first authorized Bible in English, and the Geneva Bible of 1557–1560.

The thorough Calvinism of the Geneva Bible (more evident in the marginal notes than in the translation itself) offended the High-Church party of the Church of England, to which almost all of its bishops subscribed. They associated Calvinism with Presbyterianism, which sought to replace the government of the church by bishops (Episcopalian) with the government by lay elders. However, they were aware that the Great Bible of 1539 — which was the only version then legally authorized for use in Anglican worship — was severely deficient, in that much of the Old Testament and Apocrypha was translated from the Latin Vulgate, rather than from the original Hebrew, Aramaic, and Greek. In an attempt to replace the objectionable Geneva translation, they circulated one of their own, which became known as the "Bishops' Bible".

The promoter of the exercise and the leading figure in translating was Matthew Parker, Archbishop of Canterbury. It was at his instigation that the various sections translated by Parker and his fellow bishops were followed by their initials in the early editions. For instance, at the end of the book of Deuteronomy, we find the initials "W.E.", which, according to a letter Parker wrote to Sir William Cecil, stand for William Alley, Bishop of Exeter. Parker tells Cecil that this system was "to make [the translators] more diligent, as answerable for their doings." Unhappily, Parker failed to commission anyone to act as a supervisory editor for the work completed by the various translators and was too busy to do so himself, and accordingly, translation practice varies greatly from book to book. Hence, in most of the Old Testament (as is standard in English Versions) the Tetragrammaton YHWH is represented by "the LORD", and the Hebrew "Elohim" is represented by "God". But in the Psalms, the practice is the opposite way around. The books that Parker himself worked on are fairly sparingly edited from the text of the Great Bible, while those undertaken by Grindal of London emerged much closer to the Geneva text.

The bishops deputed to revise the Apocrypha appear to have delivered very little, as the text in these books reproduce that of the Great Bible broadly the same. As the Apocrypha of the Great Bible was translated from the Latin Vulgate, the Bishops' Bible cannot strictly claim to have been entirely translated from the original tongues.

The Bishops' Bible was first published in 1568 but was then re-issued in an extensively revised form in 1572. In the revision a number of switches were made to the New Testament in the direction of more "ecclesiastical" language (e.g. introducing the term "charity" into I Corinthians 13), but otherwise to bring the text more into line with that found in the Geneva Bible; and in the Old Testament, the Psalms from the Great Bible were printed alongside those in the new translation, which had proved impossible to sing. From 1577 the new psalm translation was dropped altogether; while further incremental changes were made to the text of the New Testament in subsequent editions. The Bible had the authority of the royal warrant and was the second version appointed to be read aloud in church services (cf. Great Bible, King James Bible). It failed to displace the Geneva Bible as a domestic Bible to be read at home, but that was not its intended purpose. The intention was for it to be used in church as what would today be termed a "pulpit Bible". The version was more grandiloquent than the Geneva Bible. The first edition was exceptionally large and included 124 full-page illustrations. The second and subsequent editions were rather smaller, around the same size as the first printing of the King James Bible, and mostly lacked illustrations other than frontispieces and maps. The text lacked most of the notes and cross-references in the Geneva Bible, which contained much controversial theology, but which were helpful to people among whom the Bible was just beginning to circulate in the vernacular. The last edition of the complete Bible was issued in 1602, but the New Testament was reissued until at least 1617. William Fulke published several parallel editions up to 1633, with the New Testament of the Bishops' Bible alongside the Rheims New Testament, specifically to controvert the latter's polemical annotations. The Bishops' Bible or its New Testament went through over 50 editions, whereas the Geneva Bible was reprinted more than 150 times.

Legacy

The translators of the King James Bible were instructed to take the 1602 edition of the Bishops' Bible as their basis, although several other existing translations were taken into account. After it was published in 1611, the King James Bible soon took the Bishops' Bible's place as the de facto standard of the Church of England. Later judgments of the Bishops' Bible have not been favorable; David Daniell, in his important edition of William Tyndale's New Testament, states that the Bishops' Bible "was, and is, not loved. Where it reprints Geneva it is acceptable, but most of the original work is incompetent, both in its scholarship and its verbosity." Jack P. Lewis, in his book The Day after Domesday: The Making of the Bishops' Bible, notes that unsympathetic reviews of this Bible have been done. However, "Granting all the shortcomings eighteenth to the twenty-first-century scholarship can find in the Bishops' Bible, it was an important stage in moving English people from prohibited Bible reading to being a Bible-reading people. The revisers labored to give God's book to God's people in a language they could understand. The King James translators did not think they were making a bad translation into a good one but were making a good one better."

Unlike Tyndale's translations and the Geneva Bible, the Bishops' Bible has rarely been reprinted; however, facsimiles are available. The most available reprinting of its New Testament portion (minus its marginal notes) can be found in the fourth column of the New Testament Octapla edited by Luther Weigle, chairman of the translation committee that produced the Revised Standard Version.

The Bishops' Bible is also known as the "Treacle Bible", because of its translation of Jeremiah 8:22 which reads "Is there not treacle at Gilead?", a rendering also found in several earlier versions as well such as the Great Bible. In the Authorized Version of 1611, "treacle" was changed to "balm."[15]

---

[15] Retrieved Monday, October 21, 2019
https://en.wikipedia.org/wiki/Bishops%27_Bible

CHAPTER 13 The Douay-Rheims Bible (1582-1609)

Frederic G. Kenyon

The English exiles for religious causes were not all of one kind or of one faith. There were Roman Catholic refugees on the Continent as well as Puritan, and from the one, as from the other, there proceeded an English version of the Bible. The center of the English Roman Catholics was the English College at Douai, the foundation (in 1568) of William Allen, formerly of Queen's College, Oxford, and subsequently cardinal; and it was from this college that a new version of the Bible emanated which was intended to serve as a counterblast to the Protestant versions, with which England was now flooded. The first instalment of it appeared in 1582, during a temporary migration of the college to Rheims. This was the New Testament, the work mainly of Gregory Martin, formerly Fellow of St. John's College, Oxford, with the assistance of a small band of scholars from the same university. The Old Testament is stated to have been ready at the same time, but for want of funds it could not be printed until 1609, after the college had returned to Douai, when it appeared just in time to be of some use to the preparers of King James' version. As was natural, the Roman scholars did not concern themselves with the Hebrew and Greek originals, which they definitely rejected as inferior, but translated from the Latin Vulgate, following it with a close fidelity which is not infrequently fatal, not merely to the style, but even to the sense in English. The following short passage (Ephesians 3:6-12), taken almost at random, is a fair example of the Latinization of their style.

> The Gentils to be coheires and concorporat and comparticipant of his promis in Christ Jesus by the Gospel: whereof I am made a minister according to the gift of the grace of God, which is given me according to the operation of his power. To me the least of al the sainctes is given this grace, among the Gentils to evangelize the unsearchable riches of Christ, and to illuminate al men what is the dispensation of the sacrament hidden from worldes in God, who created al things; that the manifold wisedom of God may be notified to the Princes and Potestats in the celestials by the Church, according to the prefinition of worldes, which he made in Christ Jesus our Lord. In whom we have affiance and accesse in confidence, by the faith of him.

The translation, being prepared with a definite polemical purpose, was naturally equipped with notes of a controversial character, and with a preface in which the object and method of the work were explained. It had, however, as a whole, little success. The Old Testament was reprinted only once in the course of a century, and the New Testament not much oftener. In England the greater part of its circulation was due to the action of a vehement adversary, W. Fulke, who, in order to expose its errors, printed the Rheims New Testament in parallel columns with the Bishops' version of 1572, and the Rheims annotations with his own refutations of them; and this work had a considerable vogue. Regarded from the point of view of scholarship, the Rheims and Douai Bible is of no importance, marking retrogression rather than advance; but it needs mention in a history of the English Bible because it is one of the versions of which King James' translators made use. The Authorized Version is indeed distinguished by the strongly English (as distinct from Latin) character of its vocabulary; but of the Latin words used (and used effectively), many were derived from the Bible of Rheims and Douai.

The purpose of the version, both the text and notes, was to uphold Catholic tradition in the face of the Protestant Reformation which up till then had dominated Elizabethan religion and academic debate. As such it was an impressive effort by English Catholics to support the Counter-Reformation. The New Testament was reprinted in 1600, 1621 and 1633. The Old Testament volumes were reprinted in 1635 but neither thereafter for another hundred years. In 1589, William Fulke collated the complete Rheims text and notes in parallel columns with those of the Bishops' Bible. This work sold widely in England, being re-issued in three further editions to 1633. It was predominantly through Fulke's editions that the Rheims New Testament came to exercise a significant influence on the development of 17th century English.

Much of the text of the 1582/1610 bible employed a densely Latinate vocabulary, making it extremely difficult to read the text in places. Consequently, this translation was replaced by a revision undertaken by bishop Richard Challoner; the New Testament in three editions of 1749, 1750, and 1752; the Old Testament (minus the Vulgate apocrypha), in 1750. Although retaining the title Douay–Rheims Bible, the Challoner revision was a new version, tending to take as its base text the King James Version rigorously checked and extensively adjusted for improved readability and consistency with the Clementine edition of the Vulgate. Subsequent editions of the Challoner revision, of which there have been very many, reproduce his Old Testament of 1750 with very few changes.

Challoner's New Testament was, however, extensively revised by Bernard MacMahon in a series of Dublin editions from 1783 to 1810. These Dublin versions are the source of some Challoner bibles printed in the United States in the 19th century. Subsequent editions of the Challoner Bible printed in England most often follow Challoner's earlier New Testament texts of 1749 and 1750, as do most 20th-century printings and on-line versions of the Douay–Rheims bible circulating on the internet.

Although the Jerusalem Bible, New American Bible Revised Edition, Revised Standard Version Catholic Edition, and New Revised Standard Version Catholic Edition are the most commonly used Bibles in English-speaking Catholic churches, the Challoner revision of the Douay–Rheims often remains the Bible of choice of more-traditional English-speaking Catholics.

Other than when rendering the particular readings of the Vulgate Latin, the English wording of the Rheims New Testament follows more or less closely the Protestant version first produced by William Tyndale in 1525, an important source for the Rheims translators having been identified as that of the revision of Tyndale found in an English and Latin diglot New Testament, published by Miles Coverdale in Paris in 1538. Furthermore, the translators are especially accurate in their rendition of the definite article from Greek to English, and in their recognition of subtle distinctions of the Greek past tense, neither of which is capable of being represented in Latin. Consequently, the Rheims New Testament is much less of a new version, and owes rather more to the original languages, than the translators admit in their preface. Where the Rheims translators depart from the Coverdale text, they frequently adopt readings found in the Protestant Geneva Bible or those of the Wycliffe Bible, as this latter version had been translated from the Vulgate and had been widely used by English Catholic churchmen unaware of its Lollard origins.

Nevertheless, it was a translation of a translation of the Bible. Many highly regarded translations of the Bible routinely consult Vulgate readings, especially in certain difficult Old Testament passages; but nearly all modern Bible versions, Protestant and Catholic, go directly to original-language Hebrew, Aramaic, and Greek biblical texts as their translation base, and not to a secondary version like the Vulgate. The translators justified their preference for the Vulgate in their Preface, pointing to accumulated corruptions within the original language manuscripts available in that era, and asserting that Jerome would have had access to better manuscripts in the original tongues that had not survived. Moreover, they could point to the Council of Trent's decree that the Vulgate was, for Catholics, free of doctrinal error.

In their decision consistently to apply Latinate language, rather than everyday English, to render religious terminology, the Rheims–Douay translators continued a tradition established by Thomas More and Stephen Gardiner in their criticisms of the biblical translations of William Tyndale. Gardiner indeed had himself applied these principles in 1535 to produce a heavily revised version, which unfortunately has not survived, of Tyndale's translations of the Gospels of Luke and John. More and Gardiner had argued that Latin terms were more precise in meaning than their English equivalents, and consequently should be retained in Englished form to avoid ambiguity. However, David Norton observes that the Rheims–Douay version extends the principle much further. In the preface to the Rheims New Testament the translators criticise the Geneva Bible for their policy of striving always for clear and unambiguous readings; the Rheims translators proposed rather a rendering of the English biblical text that is faithful to the Latin text, whether or not such a word-for-word translation results in hard to understand English, or transmits ambiguity from the Latin phrasings:

> we presume not in hard places to modifie the speaches or phrases, but religiously keepe them word for word, and point for point, for feare of missing or restraining the sense of the holy Ghost to our phantasie...acknowledging with S. Hierom, that in other writings it is ynough to give in translation, sense for sense, but that in Scriptures, lest we misse the sense, we must keep the very wordes.

This adds to More and Gardiner the opposite argument, that previous versions in standard English had improperly imputed clear meanings for obscure passages in the Greek source text where the Latin Vulgate had often tended to rather render the Greek literally, even to the extent of generating improper Latin constructions. In effect, the Rheims translators argue that, where the source text is ambiguous or obscure, then a faithful English translation should also be ambiguous or obscure, with the options for understanding the text discussed in a marginal note:

> so, that people must read them with licence of their spiritual superior, as in former times they were in like sort limited. such also of the Laitie, yea & of the meaner learned Clergie, as were permitted to read holie Scriptures, did not presume to inteprete hard places, nor high Mysteries, much lesse to dispute and contend, but leaving the discussion thereof to the more learned, searched rather and noted the godlie and imitable examples of good life and so learned more humilitie, obedience...

The translation was prepared with a definite polemical purpose in opposition to Protestant translations (which also had polemical motives). Prior to the Douay-Rheims, the only printed English language Bibles available had been Protestant translations. The Tridentine–Florentine Biblical canon was naturally used, with the Deuterocanonical books incorporated into the Douay–Rheims Old Testament, and only 3 Esdras, 4 Esdras and the Prayer of Manasses in the Apocrypha section.

The translators excluded the apocryphal Psalm 151, this unusual oversight given the otherwise "complete" nature of the book is explained in passing by the annotations to Psalm 150 that "S. Augustin in the conclusion of his ... Sermons upon the Psalms, explicateth a mysterie in the number of an hundred and fieftie[.]"[16]

---

[16] Retrieved Monday, October 21, 2019
https://en.wikipedia.org/wiki/Bishops%27_Bible

CHAPTER 14 The Authorized Version (1611)

Frederic G. Kenyon

The version which was destined to put the crown on nearly a century of labor, and, after extinguishing by its excellence all rivals, to print an indelible mark on English religion and English literature, came into being almost by accident. It arose out of the Hampton Court Conference, held by James I in 1604, with the object of arriving at a settlement between the Puritan and Anglican elements in the Church; but it was not one of the prime or original subjects of the conference. In the course of discussion, Dr. Reynolds, president of Corpus Christi College, Oxford, the leader of the moderate Puritan party, referred to the imperfections and disagreements of the existing translations; and the suggestion of a new version, to be prepared by the best scholars in the country, was warmly taken up by the king. The conference, as a whole, was a failure; but James did not allow the idea of the revision to drop. He took an active part in the preparation of instructions for the work, and to him appears to be due the credit of two features which went far to secure its success. He suggested that the translation should be committed in the first instance to the universities (subject to subsequent review by the bishops and the Privy Council, which practically came to nothing), and thereby secured the services of the best scholars in the country, working in cooperation; and (on the suggestion of the bishop of London) he laid down that no marginal notes should be added, which preserved the new version from being the organ of any one party in the Church.

Ultimately it was arranged that six companies of translators should be formed, two at Westminster, two at Oxford, and two at Cambridge. The companies varied in strength from 7 to 10 members, the total (though there is some little doubt with regard to a few names) being 47. The Westminster companies undertook Genesis to 2 Kings and the Epistles, the Oxford companies the Prophets and the Gospels, Acts, and Apocalypse, and the Cambridge companies 1 Chronicles to Ecclesiastes and the Apocrypha. A series of rules was drawn up for their guidance. The Bishop's Bible was to be taken as the basis. The old ecclesiastical terms were to be kept. No marginal notes were to be affixed, except for the explanation of Hebrew or Greek words. Marginal references, on the contrary, were to be supplied. As each company finished a book, it was to send it to the other companies for their consideration. Suggestions were to be invited from the clergy generally, and opinions requested on passages of special difficulty from any learned man in the land. "These translations to be used when they agree better with the text than the Bishops' Bible, namely, Tyndale's, Matthew's, Coverdale's, Whitchurch's (i.e. the Great Bible), Geneva." The translators claim further to have consulted all the available versions and commentaries in other languages and to have repeatedly revised their own work, without grudging the time which it required. The time occupied by the whole work is stated by themselves as two years and three-quarters. The several companies appear to have begun their labors about the end of 1607 and to have taken two years in completing their several shares. A final revision, occupying nine months, was then made by a smaller body, consisting of two representatives from each company, after which it was seen through the press by Dr. Miles Smith and Bishop Bilson; and in 1611 the new version, printed by R. Barker, the king's printer, was given to the world in a large folio volume (the largest of all the series of English Bibles) of black letter type. The details of its issue are obscure. There were at least two issues in 1611, set up independently, known respectively as the "He" and "She" Bibles, from their divergence in the translation of the last words of Ruth 3:15; and bibliographers have differed as to their priority, though the general opinion is in favor of the former. [1] Some copies have a woodblock, others an engraved title-page, with different designs. The title-page was followed by the dedication to King James, which still stands in our ordinary copies of the Authorized Version, and this by the translators' preface (believed to have been written by Dr. Miles Smith), which is habitually omitted. (It is printed in the present King's Printers' Variorum Bible and is interesting and valuable both as an example of the learning of the age and for its description of the translators' labors.) For the rest, the contents and arrangement of the Authorized Version are too well known to every reader to need description.

Nor is it necessary to dwell at length on the characteristics of the translation. Not only was it superior to all its predecessors, but its excellence was so marked that no further revision was attempted for over 250 years. Its success must be attributed to the fact which differentiated it from its predecessors, namely, that it was not the work of a single scholar (like Tyndale's, Coverdale's, and Matthew's Bibles), or of a small group (like the Geneva and Douai Bibles), or of a large number of men working independently with little supervision (like the Bishops' Bible), but was produced by the collaboration of a carefully selected band of scholars, working with ample time and with full and repeated revision. Nevertheless, it was not a new translation. It owed much to its predecessors. The translators themselves say, in their preface: "We never thought from the beginning that we should need to make a new translation, nor yet to make of a bad one a good one, ... but to make a good one better, or out of many good ones one principal good one, not justly to be excepted against; that hath been our endeavor, that our mark." The description is very just. The foundations of the Authorized Version were laid by Tyndale, and a great part of his work continued through every revision. Each succeeding version added something to the original stock, Coverdale (in his own and the Great Bible) and the Genevan scholars contributing the largest share; and the crown was set upon the whole by the skilled labor of the Jacobean divines, making free use of the materials accumulated by others, and happily inspired by the gift of style which was the noblest literary achievement of the age in which they lived. A sense of the solemnity of their subject saved them from the extravagances and conceits which sometimes mar that style; and, as a result, they produced a work which, from the merely literary point of view, is the finest example of Jacobean prose, and has influenced incalculably the whole subsequent course of English literature. On the character and spiritual history of the nation it has left an even deeper mark, to which many writers have borne eloquent testimony; and if England has been, and is, a Bible-reading and Bible-loving country, it is in no small measure due to her possession of a version so nobly executed as the Authorized Version.

The history of the Authorized Version after 1611 can be briefly sketched. In spite of the name by which it is commonly known, and in spite of the statement on both title-pages of 1611 that it was "appointed to be read in churches," there is no evidence that it was ever officially authorized either by the Crown or by Convocation. Its authorization seems to have been tacit and gradual. The Bishops' Bible, hitherto the official version, ceased to be reprinted, and the Authorized Version no doubt gradually replaced it in churches as occasion arose. In domestic use, its fortunes were for a time more doubtful, and for two generations it existed concurrently with the Geneva Bible; but before the century was out its predominance was assured. The first quarto and octavo editions were issued in 1612, and thenceforth editions were so numerous that it is useless to refer to any except a few of them. The early editions were not very correctly printed. In 1638 an attempt to secure a correct text was made by a small group of Cambridge scholars. In 1633 the first edition printed in Scotland was published. In 1701 Bishop Lloyd superintended the printing of an edition at Oxford, in which Archbishop Ussher's dates for Scripture chronology were printed in the margin, where they henceforth remained. In 1717 a fine edition, printed by Baskett at Oxford, earned bibliographical notoriety as "The Vinegar Bible" from a misprint in the headline over Luke 20. [2] In 1762 a carefully revised edition was published at Cambridge under the editorship of Dr. T. Paris, and a similar edition, superintended by Dr. B. Blayney, appeared at Oxford in 1769. These two editions, in which the text was carefully revised, the spelling modernized, the punctuation corrected, and considerable alteration made in the marginal notes, formed the standard for subsequent reprints of the Authorized Version, which differ in a number of details, small in importance but fairly numerous in the aggregate, from the original text of 1611. One other detail remains to be mentioned. In 1666 appeared the first edition of the Authorized Version from which the Apocrypha was omitted. It had previously been omitted from some editions of the Geneva Bible, from 1599 onwards. The Nonconformists took much objection to it, and in 1664 the Long Parliament forbade the reading of lessons from it in public, but the lectionary of the English Church always included lessons from it. The example of omission was followed in many editions subsequently. The first edition printed in America (apart from a surreptitious edition of 1752), in 1782, is without it. In 1826 the British and Foreign Bible Society, which has been one of the principal agents in the circulation of the Scriptures throughout the world, decided never in the future to print or circulate copies containing the Apocrypha; and this decision has been carried into effect ever since.

So far as concerned the translation of the Hebrew and Greek texts which lay before them, the work of the authors of the Authorized version, as has been shown above, was done not merely well but excellently. There were, no doubt, occasional errors of interpretation; and in regard to the Old Testament, in particular, the Hebrew scholarship of the age was not always equal to the demands made upon it. But such errors as were made were not of such magnitude or quantity as to have made any extensive revision necessary or desirable even now, after a lapse of nearly three hundred years. There was, however, another defect, less important (and indeed necessarily invisible at the time), which the lapse of years ultimately forced into prominence, namely, in the text (and especially the Greek text) which they translated. As has been shown elsewhere [TEXT OF THE NEW TESTAMENT], criticism of the Greek text of the New Testament had not yet begun. Scholars were content to take the text as it first came to hand, from the late manuscripts which were most readily accessible to them. The New Testament of Erasmus, which first made the Greek text generally available in Western Europe, was based upon a small group of relatively late manuscripts, which happened to be within his reach at Basle. The edition of Stephanus in 1550, which practically established the "Received Text" which has held the field till our own day, rested upon a somewhat superficial examination of 15 manuscripts, mostly at Paris, of which only two were uncials, and these were but slightly used. None of the great manuscripts which now stand at the head of our list of authorities was known to the scholars of 1611. None of the ancient versions had been critically edited; and so far as King James' translators made use of them (as we know they did), it was as aids to interpretation, and not as evidence for the text, that they employed them. In saying this there is no imputation of blame. The materials for a critical study and restoration of the text were not then extant; and men were concerned only to translate the text which lay before them in the current Hebrew, Greek, and Latin Bibles. Nevertheless, it was in this inevitable defectiveness of text that the weakness lay which ultimately undermined the authority of the Authorized Version.

CHAPTER 15 History of the King James Version

Isaac H. Hall

THE DEMAND.

When James I. came to the throne of England, he found the Established Church in a sadly divided state. There were Conformists, who were satisfied with things as then found, and were willing to conform to existing usages; and there were Puritans, who longed for a better state of things, and were determined to have it. These parties appealed to the king, and the Puritans had great hopes that he would favor their side. In October, 1603, James therefore called a conference, to meet in Hampton Court Palace, in the coming January, "for hearing and for the determining things pretended to be amiss in the Church." So far as the objects chiefly sought were concerned, this Conference was a failure, but there began the movement for the version of the English Bible, now so widely accepted.

There were present on that occasion the leading divines, lawyers and laymen of the Church of England. Among them was Dr. John Reynolds, President of Corpus Christi College, Oxford. On the second day of the conference, this gentleman, in the course of discussion, suggested to the king, that a new version was exceedingly desirable, because of the many errors in the version then in use. That suggestion led to the action which, after some little delay, inaugurated measures for King James' version.

The Churchly party resisted the movement for a time, because they suspected some Puritan mischief to be behind it. On the other hand, the Puritan party pressed immediate action; and the king so managed affairs as to please both sides, and finally to secure their hearty cooperation. He very decidedly favored the proposition of the Puritans, but at the same time he pronounced the Genevan version to be the worst of all in the English language, and thereby pleased the Conformist party.

Arrangements for this version were completed by the appointment of fifty-four learned men, who were also to secure the suggestions of all competent persons, that, as the king put it, "our said translation may have the help and furtherance of all our principal learned men within this our kingdom." This attitude of the king, the removal of their first suspicions, and the undoubted merits of the case, brought about a hearty acquiescence on the part of those who had at first opposed the movement. His Majesty's instructions to the translators were these:

INSTRUCTIONS TO THE TRANSLATORS.

1. The ordinary Bible read in the Church, commonly called the Bishops' Bible, to be followed, and as little altered as the original will permit.

2. The names of the prophets and the holy writers, with the other names in the text, to be retained, as near as may be, accordingly as they are vulgarly used.

3. The old ecclesiastical words to be kept, as the word *church,* not to be translated *congregation.*

4. When any word hath divers significations, that to be kept which hath been most commonly used by the most eminent fathers, being agreeable to the propriety of the place and the analogies of faith.

5. The division of chapters to be altered either not at all, or as little as may be, if necessity so require.

6. No marginal notes at all to be affixed, but only for the explanation of the Hebrew or Greek words, which cannot, without some circumlocution, so briefly and fitly be expressed, in the text.

7. Such quotations of places to be marginally set down as shall serve for the fit reference of one Scripture to another.

8. Every particular man of each company to take the same chapter or chapters; and, having translated or amended them severally by himself where he thinks good, all to meet together to confirm what they have done, and agree for their part what shall stand.

9. As any one company hath dispatched any one book in this manner, they shall send it to the rest, to be considered of seriously and judiciously; for his Majesty is very careful on this point.

10. If any company, upon the review of the book so sent, shall doubt or differ upon any places, to send them word thereof, to note the places, and therewithal to send their reasons; to which if they consent not, the difference to be compounded at the general meeting, which is to be of the chief persons of each company, at the end of the work.

11. When any place of special obscurity is doubted of, letters to be directed by authority to send to any learned man in the land for his judgment of such a place.

12. Letters to be sent from every bishop to the rest of his clergy, admonishing them of this translation in hand, and to move and charge as many as, being skillful in the tongues, have taken pains in that kind, to send their particular observations to the company, either at Westminster, Cambridge, or Oxford, according as it was directed before in the king's letter to the archbishop.

13. The directors in each company to be the Deans of Westminster and Chester, for Westminster, and the king's professors in Hebrew and Greek in the two universities.

14. These translations to be used, when they agree better with the text than the Bishops' Bible: Tyndale's, Coverdale's, Matthew's [Rogers'], Whitchurch's [Cranmer's], Geneva."

15. By a later rule, "three or four of the most ancient and grave divines, in either of the universities, not employed in translating, to be assigned to be overseers of the translation, for the better observation of the fourth rule."

Only forty-seven of the men appointed for this work are known to have engaged in it. These were divided into six companies, two of which met at Oxford, two at Cambridge, and two at Westminster. They were presided over severally by the Dean of Westminster and by the two Hebrew Professors of the Universities.

To the first company, at Westminster (ten in number), was assigned the Old Testament as far as 2 Kings; the second company (seven in number) had the Epistles. The first company at Cambridge (numbering eight) had 2 Chronicles to Ecclesiastes; the second company (numbering seven) had the Apocryphal books. To the first Oxford company (seven in number) were assigned the prophetical books, from Isaiah to Malachi; to the second (eight in number) were given the four Gospels, the Acts and the Apocalypse, or Revelation.

A few of the principal men among those learned translators were these:

- Dr. Launcelot Andrewes, Dean of Westminster, presided over the Westminster company. Fuller says of him: "The world wanted learning to know how learned this man was, so skilled in all (especially Oriental) languages, that some conceive he might, if then living, almost have served as an interpreter-general at the confusion of tongues." He became successively Bishop of Chichester, Ely and Winchester. Born 1555, died 1626.

- Dr. Edward Lively, Regius Professor of Hebrew at Cambridge, and thus at the head of the Cambridge company, was eminent for his knowledge of Oriental languages, especially of Hebrew. He died in 1605, having been Professor of Hebrew for twenty-five years. His death was a great loss to the work which he had helped to begin, but not to complete.

- Dr. John Overall was made Professor of Divinity at Cambridge in 1596, and in 1604 was Dean of St. Paul's, London. He was considered by some the most scholarly divine in England. In 1614 he was made Bishop of Litchfield and Coventry. He was transferred to the See of Norwich in 1618. Born 1559, died 1619.

- Dr. Adrian de Saravia is said to have been the only foreigner employed on the work. He was born in Artois, France; his Father was a Spaniard, and his mother a Belgian. In 1582 he was Professor of Divinity at Leyden; in 1587 he came to England. He became Prebend of Canterbury, and afterward Canon of Westminster. He was noted for his knowledge of Hebrew. Born 1531, died 1612.

- William Bedwell, or Beadwell, was one of the greatest Arabic scholars of his day. At his death he left unfinished MSS. of an Arabic Lexicon, and also of a Persian Dictionary.

- Dr. Laurence Chadderton was for thirty-eight years Master of Emanuel College, Cambridge, and well versed in Rabbinical learning. He was one of the few Puritan divines among the translators. Born 1537; died 1640, at the advanced age of one hundred and three.

- Dr. John Reynolds, who first suggested the work, was a man of great attainments in Hebrew and Greek. He died before the revision was completed, but worked at it during his last sickness as long as his strength permitted. Born 1549, died 1607.

- Dr. Richard Kilbye, Oxford Professor of Hebrew, was reckoned among the first Hebraists of his day. Died 1620.

- Dr. Miles Smith was a student of classic authors from his youth, was well acquainted with the Rabbinical learning, and well versed in Hebrew, Chaldee, Syriac and Arabic. He was often called a "walking library." Born about 1568, died 1624.

- John Boyse, or Bois, at six years of age could write Hebrew elegantly. He was for twelve years chief lecturer in Greek at St. John's College, Cambridge. Bishop Andrewes, of Ely, made him a prebend in his church in 1615. He was one of the most laborious of all the revisers. Born 1560, died 1643.

- Sir Henry Saville was warden of Merton College, Oxford, for thirty-six years. He devoted his fortune to the encouragement of learning, and was himself a fine Greek scholar. Born 1549, died 1622.

- Dr. Thomas Holland was Regius Professor of Divinity in Exeter College, Oxford, and also Master of his college. He was considered a prodigy in all branches of literature. Born 1539, died 1612.

COMPLETION OF THE REVISION.

Some work upon the revision was, in all probability, begun soon after the appointment of the committees. Vigorous effort was, however, delayed till about 1607, for what reason is unknown.

When the translators had finished their work, a copy each was sent from Oxford, Cambridge and Westminster to London, where two from each place, six in all, gave it a final revision, and Dr. Miles Smith and Bishop Wilson superintended the work as it passed through the press. The former wrote the Preface, which is entitled, "The Translators to the Reader."

The expenses of the work were not borne by the king, who pleaded poverty, but by voluntary contributions from bishops and others who had fat livings. The king, however, rewarded the translators by bestowing good livings on them as vacancies occurred, and by ecclesiastical promotion.

The work was given to the public in 1611, in a folio volume printed in black letter, the full title as follows:

"The | HOLY | BIBLE, | Conteyning the Old Testament, | AND THE NEW, | Newly Translated out of the Original | tongues: & with the former Translations | diligently compared and revised by his | Maiesties special Comandement. | Appointed to be read in Churches | Imprinted at London by Robert | Barker, Printer to the Kings | most excellent Maiestie | Anno Dom. 1611."

The same year, the New Testament, in 12mo, was issued, and in 1612, the entire Bible in 8vo, and in Roman type. The Genevan Bible, however, had a firm hold on the popular heart, and it required the lifetime of a generation to displace it.

This "Authorized Version" never was authorized by royal proclamation, by order of Council, by act of Parliament or by vote of Convocation. Whether the words "appointed to be read in churches" were used by order of the editors, or by the will of the printer, is unknown. The original manuscripts of this work are wholly lost, no trace of them having been discovered since about 1655.

The title-page speaks of this version as being "with the former translations diligently compared and revised." In their address to the readers, the translators themselves say: "Truly, we never thought, from the beginning ... that we should need to make a new translation, nor yet to make of a bad one a good one; but to make a good one better, or out of many good ones, one principal good one." Speaking of this acknowledgment, Dr. Krauth, of the present version committee, says: "Without this confession, the Authorized Version would tell its own story. It is only necessary to compare it with the older versions, to see that with much that is original, with many characteristic beauties, in some of which no other translation approaches it, it is yet in the main a revision. Even its original beauties are often the mosaic of an exquisite combination of the fragments of the older. Comparing it with the English exemplars it follows, we must say it is not the fruit of their bloom, but the ripeness of their fruit."

The singular fact has been brought to light within a few years that in the year 1611 there were two distinct folio editions of this Bible published. There are some copies extant where the sheets from the two are combined; and some, where the title-page of 1611 is prefixed to the later editions. The two editions of 1611 had distinctive titles, though it is said that in some cases these were interchanged; one being a wood-cut which had been used before in the earlier Bishops' Bible, and the other an elegant copperplate. Each of them has also errors and readings peculiar to itself. One edition has, for instance, "Judas" instead of "Jesus" in Matt. xxvi., 36; the other has a part of the verse repeated in Exod. xiv., 10, making what printers call "a doublet." In Gen. x., 16, one copy reads the "Emorite," and the other the "Amorite." One has in Ruth iii., 15, "He went into the city;" the other has, "She went into the city." This led to their being designated, the great He Bible, and the great She Bible.

WINNING ITS WAY.

King James made great promises concerning his new version. He said at the outset that it "should be ratified by royal authority and adopted for exclusive use in all the churches." The title-page set forth that the work was by "His Maiesties special Commandement;" also that it is "appointed to be read in churches;" and finally, that it comes from the press of "Robert Barker, printer to the King's most excellent Maiestie." All this parade seems to guarantee some civil force to urge the new version into general use, but so far as can be learned from history, the book was left to win its way upon its merits alone. Indeed it was not until 1661, that the Epistles and the Gospels in the Prayer Book, were changed, the authorized text superseding that of the Bishops' Bible. The Psalms in the Prayer Book, from the "Bible of largest volume in English," have not been superseded to this day.

EXCELLENCE OF KING JAMES' VERSION.

The Rev. Dr. Talbot W. Chambers, himself one of the revisers of the Old Testament Company, has very beautifully and truly said of the King James' Version as follows: "The merits of the Authorized Version, in point of fidelity to the original, are universally acknowledged. No other version, ancient or modern, surpasses it, save, perhaps, the Dutch, which was made subsequently, and profited by the labors of the English translators. But a version may be faithful without being elegant. It may be accurate without adequately representing the riches of the language in which it is made. The glory of the English Bible is that while it conveys the mind of the Spirit with great exactness, it does this in such a way that the book has become the highest existing standard of our noble tongue. Lord Macaulay calls it a stupendous work, which, if everything else in our language should perish, would alone suffice to show the whole extent of its beauty and power."

Mr. Huxley, whose tendency to superstitious reverence will not be suspected, has said of this version: "It is written in the noblest and purest English, and abounds in exquisite beauties of mere literary form." The style used in this version was unique. It was not the English of that day, either spoken or written. Indeed, Mr. Marsh, in his "Lectures on the English Language" asserts, that the dialect used was not at any period "the actual current book language, nor the colloquial speech of the English people."

The fact concerning the style of this version is, that from the earliest effort at English version each succeeding translator improved upon his predecessors, taking his best points continually, so that in the end the chief excellence of each appeared. King James' version, therefore, combines the beautiful and felicitous expression of all who went before it.

As a final testimony to the excellence of the King James' version we may quote from Dr. F. W. Faber, who says: "Who will say that the uncommon beauty and marvelous English of the Protestant Bible is not one of the great strongholds against heresy in this country? It lives on the ear, like music that can never be forgotten, like the sound of church bells, which the convert hardly knows how he can forego. Its felicities often seem to be almost things rather than words. It is part of the national mind, and the anchor of national seriousness. Nay, it is worshiped with a positive idolatry, in extenuation of whose grotesque fanaticism its intrinsic beauty pleads availingly with the man of letters and the scholar. The memory of the dead passes into it. The potent traditions of childhood are stereotyped in its verses. The power of all the griefs and trials of a man are hid beneath its words. It is the representative of his best moments, and all that there has been about him of soft and gentle, and pure and penitent and good, speaks to him forever out of his Protestant Bible. It is a sacred thing which doubt has never dimmed, and controversy never soiled."

CHAPTER 16 How the King James Version Became Popular

Edward D. Andrews

2011 was the year of the 400th anniversary of the King James version of the Bible, otherwise known as the *Authorized Version*. The English-speaking world was in full celebration. Leland Ryken and Crossway Publishing began the year with the new release *The Legacy of the King James Bible: Celebrating 400 Years of the Most Influential English Translation* (January 5, 2011). There were television and radio specials, documentaries, as well as conferences, lectures, and seminars. King James I of England produced the translation that is noted for its "majesty of style," and has been labeled as one of the most important books in the English history[17] and a driving force that shaped the English-speaking world.[18]

> The King James Bible is a book that attracts superlatives. To David Norton it is "the most important book in English religion and culture," to Gordon Campbell "the most celebrated book in the English-speaking world" and "the most enduring embodiment of Scripture in the English language". To Robert Carroll and Stephen Prickett, it is simply the Bible translation that defines Bible translations: "All other versions still exist, as it were, in its shadow. It has shaped, formed and moulded the language with which the others must speak."[19]

How, though, did the King James Bible attain such a unique place in the hearts and minds of the English-speaking people?

Bible Translation Increases Momentum

Around 1550 there was a yearning for the knowledge of the teachings of the Bible, which had begun to sweep across Europe. John Wycliffe (1330? - 84), a Catholic priest and a professor of theology at Oxford, England had whetted the appetite of English-speaking people almost two centuries earlier, about 1380, with a handwritten translation of the Bible from Latin. Over the next two centuries, the followers of Wycliffe, known

---

[17] The Times Literary Supplement. 9 February 2011. Archived from the original on 2011-06-17. Retrieved July 30, 2018.

[18] "The King James Bible: The Book That Changed the World - BBC Two". BBC

[19] The Times Literary Supplement. 9 February 2011. Archived from the original on 2011-06-17. Retrieved July 30, 2018.

as the Lollards, **circulated his Bible texts countrywide**, determined than ever to keep Wycliffe's work alive. The nickname "Lollard" had its origin going back to the 14th century in the Netherlands. However, Wycliffe died, this name truly came to the fore. It originated from the Middle Dutch lullen (from which we get the English word "lull," archaically meaning to sing, hum or chant), and thus denotes 'a praiser of God.'

Bible scholar and translator William Tyndale's New Testament was yet another breakthrough. The Tyndale Bible was translated from the original Greek language into English by 1525, being the first printed translation. On the heels of Tyndale, Miles Coverdale came out with the complete English Bible in 1535. One year prior to that Henry VIII broke off his relationship with Rome and also made a decisive move. Seeking to strengthen his position as head of the Church of England, Henry VIII commissioned a translation of the Bible into English, which became the first authorized edition of the Bible in English. Because of its immense size (11 inches wide by 16½ inches long in heavy Gothic type), it became known as the Great Bible.

The Puritans and other Protestants, who were exiled from all over Europe settled in Geneva, Switzerland. In 1560 the Geneva Bible, the first English Bible the first Bible to shun the use of Old English Black Gothic type (easy-to-read type) was produced with chapters divided into verses. The Geneva Bible was the first Bible to be printed in a handy size. It was shipped to England from continental Europe and immediately became popular. The Geneva Bible was eventually printed in England as well. Maps, as well as marginal notes, which notes could be found on essentially every page of the Bible, served to help clarify its text. There was some opposition to these notes, however, because they spoke against the papacy.

Overcoming the Difficulties

The Great Bible never really gained widespread acceptance. The Geneva Bible included voluminous hostile footnotes to the papacy. Therefore, a revised Bible was decided upon. the Great Bible was chosen as its foundation. The task was given to Church of England bishops, and in 1568 the Bishops' Bible was published. This two was a large edition, filled with many engravings. However, it too was short-lived and not well-received in England because the Calvinists, who spurned religious titles, objected to the word "bishops."

King James I ascended the English throne in 1603; thereafter, he endorsed the making of a fresh Bible translation. He wanted to make it available to all omitting any offensive notes or comments.

King James backed the project. Ultimately, 47 scholars in six separate groups throughout the country prepared segments of the text. The translation committee made use of Both the Tyndale and the Coverdale Bibles. The Tyndale New Testament was about 84 percent of the text, while in the Old Testament about 76 percent. Most King James Bible users today do not realize that it was a revision of earlier English translations. It was basically a revision of the Bishops' Bible. However, they also used the Geneva Bible and the Roman Catholic Rheims New Testament of 1582.

The **King James Version (KJV)**, also known as the **King James Bible** (KJB) or simply the Authorized **Version** (AV), is an English translation of the Christian **Bible** for the Church of England, begun in 1604 and completed in May of 1611. James himself was a respected Bible scholar, and the translation's dedication acknowledge his leadership, "the most high and mighty prince, James, by the grace of God, king of Great Britain, France, and Ireland, Defender of the Faith, etc." is given credit for having by means of a tract dealt "such a blow to that Man of Sin [meaning the pope] as will not be healed."[20] It was perceived at that time that James, as the head of the Church of England, was seen to be exerting his authority to bring the nation together.

A Literary Masterpiece

The clergy was very pleased to receive this so-called authorized version from the hand of their king. "It was issued in a large folio, in double columns, **with the title** 'The Holy Bible, conteyning the Old Testament, and the New: Newly Translated out of the Originall tongues: and with the former Translations diligently compared and revised by his Maiesties speciall Commandement. Appointed to be read in Churches.' The printer was Robert Barker, London."[21] Yet, even then, how would the nation receive this new translation, seeing that those that came before it never took hold for various reasons.

The translators themselves expressed their apprehension as to its success in an extended preface. The Geneva Bible was the most well received up unto this point; thus, it took 30 years for the King James Bible to displace the Geneva Bible in the affections of the people.

---

[20] William Hendriksen and Simon J. Kistemaker, *Exposition of I-II Thessalonians*, vol. 3, New Testament Commentary (Grand Rapids: Baker Book House, 1953–2001), 174.

[21] Edward Maunde Thompson, *Bible Illustrations* (Oxford; London: Oxford University Press; Henry Frowde, 1896), 38.

The *Cambridge History of the Bible* concludes: "Strictly speaking, the Authorized Version was never authorized, nor were parish churches ordered to procure it. It replaced the Bishops' Bible in public use because after 1611 no other folio Bible was printed. But from Broughton onwards it met with plenty of criticism. In ordinary private use the comprehensive Geneva Bible long competed with it, while scholars and preachers went on using what they would. So strong a Protestant as Becon had continued to quote the Vulgate in Latin or translate directly from it, while at times he took up Tyndale or the Great Bible apparently as it came to hand. Later, so prominent a reviser as Lancelot Andrewes commonly used the Geneva Bible for his sermons, as did other bishops. Eventually, however, its victory [the King James Version] was so complete that its text acquired a sanctity properly ascribable only to the unmediated voice of God; to multitudes of English-speaking Christians it has seemed little less than blasphemy to tamper with the words of the King James Version."[22]

Acts 1:8 "To the Uttermost Part of the Earth"

When the early settlers landed in North America they had the Geneva Bible in hand. However, in time the King James Version would take over and gain far greater acceptance. Moreover, with the expansion of the British Empire throughout the world, so too, Protestant missionaries spread its use. This author is in South America at the time of the writing of this book and I just discovered some very interesting news about the Baptist seminary in Chile, who claim to be of the Southern Baptist Convention position. They only use the Textus Receptus (the text behind the King James Version) and refuse to let their students even use the critical texts WH-NU[23] (the text behind modern translations). The Baptist Church that I attend has a pastor that uses only the King James Version, while his assistant pastor sneaks to use the critical text. Many throughout the last century have translated the Bible into local languages were unfamiliar with Biblical Hebrew and Greek. Therefore, the *King James Version* in English became the source for these local translations.

According to the British Library today, "**The King James Bible remains the most widely published text in the English language.** The official language of the medieval Church was Latin - the language of the Roman Empire. In England, since the early 1400s, it was strictly forbidden to

---

[22] S. L. Greenslade, *The Cambridge History of the Bible, Vol. 3: The West from the Reformation to the Present Day*, (Cambridge University Press, Cambridge, 1975), 168.

[23] Wescott and Hort Critical Text, the Nestle-Aland Critical text, and the United Bible Societies Critical Text.

translate the Bible into English. Tyndale's translation of the bible in 1525 had led to his execution. But by Shakespeare's time, England had split with Rome, and the political scenery had changed. Bibles in English were now available, such as Henry VIII's authorised 'Great Bible'. King James I abolished the death penalty attached to English Bible translation and commissioned a new version that would use the best available translations and sources, and importantly, be free of biased footnotes and commentaries."[24] Some have estimated that the number of copies of the King James Version that have been produced in print worldwide is over one billion!

The Need for Change

There has been a level that runs from devotion to a translation they only know to the other extreme of cult worship of the King James Version. It began with the critical text the Textus Receptus (Latin: "Received Text") behind the New Testament of the King James Version. Desiderius Erasmus' new work was published by Froben of Basel in 1516. It was given such reverence that for several hundred years, even though new original language Greek manuscripts came to light, which dated centuries earlier than the handful of very late Byzantine manuscripts used by Erasmus, no textual scholar dare make corrections to the master Greek text. Harold Greenlee writes, "The Textus Receptus did indeed become the generally received text for nearly three hundred years, as well as the basis for the translation of the early English versions, including the KJV, and various versions in other European languages."[25]

Bruce Metzger writes, "the Textus Receptus lies at the basis of the King James Version and of all the principal Protestant translations prior to 1881. So superstitious has been the reverence accorded the Textus Receptus that in some cases attempts to criticize or emend it has been regarded as akin to sacrilege. Yet, its textual basis is essentially a handful of late and haphazardly collected minuscule manuscripts, and in dozens of passages its rendering is supported by no known Greek witnesses [manuscripts]."[26] In the 19th century, enough time chad passed, so "the influential edition [of the critical Greek Text of the New Testament] prepared by two Cambridge scholars,

---

[24] THE BRISTISH LIBRARY: Learning Timelines: Sources from History (Wednesday, August 01, 2018) http://www.bl.uk/learning/timeline/item102771.html

[25] Greenlee, J. Harold. *The Text of the New Testament: From Manuscript to Modern Edition* (p. 48). Baker Publishing Group.

[26] Bruce Metzger and Bart D. Ehrman, *THE TEXT OF THE NEW TESTAMENT: Its Transmission, Corruption, and Restoration* (4th Edition) (New York, NY: Oxford University Press, 2005), 152.

B. F. Westcott and F. J. A. Hort (1881). It is the latter edition that was taken as the basis for the present United Bible Societies' edition. During the twentieth century, with the discovery of several New Testament manuscripts much older than any that had hitherto been available, it has become possible to produce editions of the New Testament that approximate ever more closely to what is regarded as the wording of the original documents."[27]

In 1881, we have the B. F. Westcott and F. J. A. Hort (1881) master Greek text that displaces the long-revered Textus Receptus. We also have in 1870, work on a full revision of the King James Version started in England. We end up with both the English Revised Version of 1881 and the American Standard Version of 1901. More recent revisions of the King James Version would be the 1952 Revised Standard Version, the 1982 Revised Authorised Version, the 1985 New American Standard Bible, in 1989 the New Revised Standard Version, and the 2001 English Standard Version are all revisions of the King James Version. In 1901, the preface to the American Standard Version said, "We are not insensible to the justly lauded beauty and vigor of the style of the Authorized Version."[28] In 1982, the preface to the Revised Authorised Version said that effort was made "to maintain that lyrical quality which is so highly regarded in the Authorised Version"[29] of 1611. In 1989, the preface to the New Revised Standard Version said, "to summarize in a single sentence: the New Revised Standard Version of the Bible is an authorized revision of the Revised Standard Version, published in 1952, which was a revision of the American Standard Version, published in 1901, which, in turn, embodied earlier revisions of the King James Version, published in 1611."[30]

In 2001, the preface to the English Standard Version said, "The English Standard Version (ESV) stands in the classic mainstream of English Bible translations over the past half-millennium. The fountainhead of that stream was William Tyndale's New Testament of 1526; marking its course were the King James Version of 1611 (KJV), the English Revised Version of 1885 (RV), the American Standard Version of 1901 (ASV), and the Revised Standard Version of 1952 and 1971 (RSV). In that stream, faithfulness to the text and vigorous pursuit of precision were combined with simplicity,

---

[27] Bruce Manning Metzger, United Bible Societies, *A Textual Commentary on the Greek New Testament*, Second Edition a Companion Volume to the United Bible Societies' Greek New Testament (4th Rev. Ed.) (London; New York: United Bible Societies, 1994), xxiv.

[28] American Standard Version (Oak Harbor, WA: Logos Research Systems, Inc., 1995).

[29] The Holy Bible: Revised Authorised Version (Samuel Bagster, 1982).

[30] The Holy Bible: New Revised Standard Version (Nashville: Thomas Nelson Publishers, 1989).

beauty, and dignity of expression. Our goal has been to carry forward this legacy for this generation and generations to come."[31] There is little doubt that the King James Version is a literary masterpiece, which this author has and will appreciate and value for its unparalleled beauty of expression. This book is in no way trying to take away from what the King James Version has accomplished. However, what about the importance of its message? Is it the most accurate translation? Should it be trusted above all others?

From the 1901 American Standard Version to the 1952 Revised Standard Version, to the 1982 Revised Authorised Version, the 1985 New American Standard Bible, and the 2001 English Standard Version, the translation committees and publishers wanted to hold onto the legacy of the King James Version. Yet, these translations all have one thing in common, all made one common significant adjustment. "During the twentieth century [and now twenty-first century], with the discovery of several New Testament manuscripts much older than any that had hitherto been available, it has become possible to produce editions of the New Testament that approximate ever more closely to what is regarded as the wording of the original documents."[32]

A Valuable Modern Translation

This author's primary purpose is to give the Bible readers what God said by way of his human authors, not reverence or even worship of one translation that is itself an admitted revision of other translations in its place, as Truth Matters! The primary goal is to guide the reader to the most accurate and faithful translation, ones that are mirror-like reflections of the originally inspired Word of God. Translating Truth! The Updated American Standard Version will be one of the most faithful and accurate translations to date. www.uasvbible.org/

Chapter 17 will now take on the question found in on many Christian minds whether they use the King James Version or any modern Bible translation. Why have modern Bible translations removed many words, sentences, and verses that are in the King James Bible? When I say this question and the answers are a matter of eternal life and eternal death, it is not hyperbole.

---

[31] The Holy Bible: English Standard Version (Wheaton: Standard Bible Society, 2016).

[32] Bruce Manning Metzger, United Bible Societies, A Textual Commentary on the Greek New Testament, Second Edition a Companion Volume to the United Bible Societies' Greek New Testament (4th Rev. Ed.) (London; New York: United Bible Societies, 1994), xxiv.

CHAPTER 17 Modern Bible Translations Have Been Accused of Removing Words, Phrases, Sentences, Who Verses, Even Whole Sections

Edward D. Andrews

The Warning

Deuteronomy 4:2; 12:32 Updated American Standard Version (UASV)

[2] You shall not add to the word which I am commanding you, nor take away from it, that you may keep the commandments of Jehovah your God which I command you. [32] "Everything that I command you, you shall be careful to do; you shall not add to nor take away from it.

Revelation 22:18-19 Updated American Standard Version (UASV)

[18] I testify to everyone who hears the words of the prophecy of this book: if anyone adds to them, God will add to him the plagues which are written in this book; [19] and if anyone takes away from the words of the book of this prophecy, God will take away his part from the tree of life and out of the holy city, which are written in this book.

These are the verses that the King James Version Onlyist use to misinform the King James Version reader. First, it is true that if one removes a part of the Bible that was in the originals, it would be a catastrophic mater for that person or persons. Second, I would argue, as would the modern-day translators, that Luke 17:36 under discussion herein, as well as Matthew 18:11; 23:14 were not in the originals, they were added by later copyists, who are actually the ones who added to God's Word and so, they face the above judgment. Third, I would further point out that you cannot add what was never there in the first place. Let us see why the modern-day Bibles are not lacking these verses. Because this may be the first time some are hearing that there are certain words, phrases, sentences, even whole verses that are found in the King James Version and other older translations that are not authentic, i.e., they were not in the original.

Before we begin, let's make it clear that the entire Bible that we have today, the critical translation of the Hebrew Old Testament and the Greek New Testament are mirror-like reflections of the originals. All translations that remain faithful to the original are reliable. New Testament textual scholars have over 5,836+ Greek manuscripts, not to mention ancient versions such as Latin, Coptic, Syriac, Armenian, Georgian, and Gothic, which number into the tens of thousands. We have many early and reliable manuscripts in Greek and the versions, a good number that cover almost the entire New Testament dating within 100 years of the originals. Therefore, reconstructing the original Greek New Testament is not only realistic but is now a reality.

Copying Manuscripts

Some are still not aware that no Bible translator has had access to the originals of the New Testament when making their translations because they have not been in existence for almost 2,000 years. Even if they were discovered, we could never ascertain that they were the originals unless they were autographed by Matthew, Mark, Luke, John, James, Peter, or Jude. Almost immediately after the originals were written, copies were being made to be used by the early Christian church.

We have inherited from the past generation the view that the early text was a 'free' text, and the discovery of the Chester Beatty papyri seemed to confirm this view. When P^{45} and P^{46} were joined by P^{66} sharing the same characteristics, this position seemed to be definitely established. P^{75} appeared in contrast to be a loner with its "strict" text anticipating Codex Vaticanus. Meanwhile, the other witnesses of the early period had been ignored. It is their collations which have changed the picture so completely.[33]

While we have said this once, it bears repeating, as *some* of the earliest manuscripts that we now have evidence that a professional scribe copied them. *Many* of the other papyri confirm that a semiprofessional hand copied them, while *most* of these early papyri give evidence of being produced by a copyist who was literate and experienced. Therefore, either literate or semiprofessional copyist did the vast majority of the early extant papyri, with some being done by professionals. As it happened, the few poorly copied manuscripts became known first, establishing a precedent that was difficult for some to shake when the enormous amount of evidence emerged that showed just the opposite.

The most reliable of the earliest texts are P^1, $P^{4, 64, 67}$, P^{23}, P^{27}, P^{30}, P^{32}, P^{35}, $P^{39, P49, 65}$, P^{70}, P^{75}, P^{86}, P^{87}, P^{90}, P^{91}, P^{100}, P^{101}, P^{106}, P^{108}, P^{111}, P^{114}, and P^{115}. The copyists of these manuscripts allowed very few variants in their copies of the exemplars. They had the ability to make accurate judgments as they

---

[33] (Aland and Aland, The Text of the New Testament 1995, 93-5)

went about their copying, resulting in superior texts. Whether their skills in copying were a result of their belief that they were copying a sacred text, or from their training, cannot be known. It could have been a combination of both. These papyri are of great importance when considering textual problems and are considered by many textual scholars to be a good representation of the original wording of the text that was first published by the biblical author. Still, "many of these manuscripts contain singular readings and some 'Alexandrian' polishing, which needs to be sifted out." (P. Comfort 2005, 269) Nevertheless, again, they are the best texts and the most faithful in preserving the original. While it is true that some of the papyri are mere fragments, some contain substantial portions of text. We should note too that text types really did not exist per se in the second century, and it is a mere convention to refer to the papyri as Alexandrian, since the best Alexandrian manuscript, Vaticanus, did exist in the second century by way of P^{75}. It is not that the Alexandrian text existed, but rather P^{75}/Vaticanus evidence that some very strict copying with great care was taking place. Manuscripts that were not of this caliber of strict and careful copying were the result of scribal errors and scribes taking liberties with the text. Therefore, even though P^5 may be categorized as a Western text-type, it is more a matter of negligence in the copying process.

"What we do know, from the manuscript evidence, is that several of the earliest Christian scribes were well-trained scribes who applied their training to making reliable texts, both of the Old Testament and the New Testament. We know that they were conscientious to make a reliable text in the process of transcription (as can been seen in manuscripts like $P^{4+64+67}$ and P^{75}), and we know that others worked to rid the manuscript of textual corruption. This is nowhere better manifested than in P^{66}, where the scribe himself and the *diorthotes* (official corrector) made over 450 corrections to the text of John. As is explained in the next chapter, the *diorthotes* of P^{66} probably consulted other exemplars (one whose text was much like that of P^{75}) in making his corrections. This shows a standard Alexandrian scriptoral practice at work in the reproduction of a New Testament manuscript." (P. Comfort, Encountering the Manuscripts: An Introduction to New Testament Paleography and Textual Criticism 2005, 264)

Scribes Taking Liberties

While we can say that the early Alexandrian copyists certainly made some mistakes at times and added some intentional changes, generally, they used extreme care to make certain that their work was an exact duplication of the exemplar (archetype; master copy) that they were copying. Metzger tells us of another family of manuscripts, "The *Byzantine text*, otherwise called the *Syrian text* (so Westcott and Hort), ..., on the whole, the latest of the several distinctive types of text of the New Testament. It is characterized chiefly by lucidity and completeness. The framers of this text sought to smooth away any harshness of language, to combine two or more divergent readings into one expanded reading (called conflation), and to harmonize divergent parallel passages. This conflated text, produced perhaps at Antioch in Syria, was taken to Constantinople, whence it was distributed widely throughout the Byzantine Empire."[34]

It went something like this, a scribe who was very familiar with the Gospel of Matthew, as he is going about the work of copying the Gospel of Mark or Luke, had a tendency to to pen the wording that he had memorized from Matthew. Another way these interpolations crept into the text was carried out unintentionally as well. The scribe who is familiar with the Gospels may take note that a sentence that Matthew used was not to be found in Mark or Luke, so the scribe decides to add the sentence into the margin. However, a later copyist using this manuscript as his exemplar might not know if the sentence that has been added to the margin is there because it should be in the main text, so he moves the sentence from the margin to the main text in his copy of Mark or Luke, as it makes the accounts agree more closely. For example, In Luke's account of the Lord's Prayer, some manuscripts (A C D W Θ Ψ 070 f[13] 33[vid] Maj it syr[c,h,p] cop) add "Our Father who is in heaven"[35] (Luke 11:2a) Also, in Luke 11:2b, which should read "let your kingdom come," some manuscripts (D it[d]) expand it to, "let your kingdom come **upon us**."[36] In addition, in Luke 11:2c, some manuscripts (א A C D W Θ Ψ 070 f 33 Maj it syr[p] cop[bo]) add "let your will be done on earth as it is in heaven," which is not present in (P[75] B L syr[c,] Marcion Origen).[37] The weightier manuscript evidence suggests that this interpolation was taken from Matthew 6:10. These harmonizations were interpolations from sincerely motivated scribes with good intentions.

---

[34] Bruce Manning Metzger, United Bible Societies, *A Textual Commentary on the Greek New Testament, Second Edition a Companion Volume to the United Bible Societies' Greek New Testament (4th Rev. Ed.)* (London; New York: United Bible Societies, 1994), xxi.

[35] Philip W. Comfort, *New Testament Text and Translation Commentary: Commentary on the Variant Readings of the Ancient New Testament Manuscripts and How They Relate to the Major English Translations* (Carol Stream, IL: Tyndale House Publishers, Inc., 2008), 202.

[36] IBID., 202.

[37] IBID., 203.

The Dark Ages (5th to 15th centuries C.E.), was a time when the Church had the Bible locked up in the Latin language, and scholarship and learning were nearly nonexistent. However, with the birth of the Morning Star of the Reformation, John Wycliffe (1328-1384), and the invention of the printing press in 1455, the restraints were loosened, and there was a rebirth of interest in the Greek language. Moreover, with the fall of Constantinople to the Turks in 1453 C. E., many Greek scholars and their manuscripts were scattered abroad, resulting in a revival of Greek in the Western citadels of learning. Now, let us jump ahead to the 16th century, just prior to the plethora of English translations that were to come on the scene. After the invention of the Guttenberg printing press in 1455, it would be this Byzantine text which would become the first printed edition by way of Desiderius Erasmus in 1516. Thanks to an advertisement by the publishers it was referred to as the Textus Receptus, or the "Received Text." The Scriptures had been locked up in the Latin language for a thousand years and now scholars began to demand copies in Greek, the language in which the New Testament was written.

About fifty years later, or at the beginning of the sixteenth century, Ximenes, archbishop of Toledo, Spain, a man of rare capability and honor, invited foremost scholars of his land to his university at Alcala to produce a multiple-language Bible—not for the common people, but for the educated. The outcome would be the Polyglot, named Complutensian, corresponding to the Latin of Alcala. This would be a Bible of six large volumes, beautifully bound, containing the Old Testament in four languages (Hebrew, Aramaic, Greek, and Latin) and the New Testament in two (Greek and Latin). For the Greek New Testament, these scholars had only a few manuscripts available to them, and those of late origin. One may wonder why this was the case when they were supposed to have access to the Vatican library. This Bible was completed in 1514, providing the first printed Greek New Testament, but it did not receive approval by the pope to be published until 1520 and was not released to the public until 1522.

Froben, a printer in Basel, Switzerland became aware of the completion of the Complutensian Polyglot Bible and of its pending consent by the pope to be published. Immediately, he saw a prospect of making profits. He at once sent word to Erasmus, who was the foremost European scholar of the day and whose works he had published in Latin, pleading with him to hurry through a Greek New Testament text. In an attempt to bring the first published Greek text to completion, Erasmus was only able to locate, in July of 1515, a few late cursive manuscripts for collating and preparing his text. It would go to press in October of 1515 and would be completed by March of 1516. In fact, Erasmus was in such a hurried mode that he rushed the manuscript containing the Gospels to the printer without first editing it, making such changes as he felt were necessary on the proof sheets. Because of this terrible rush job, the work contained hundreds of typographical errors, as we noted earlier. Erasmus himself admitted this in his preface, remarking that it was "rushed through rather than edited." Bruce Metzger referred to the Erasmian text as a "debased form of the Greek Testament." (B. M. Metzger 1964, 1968, 1992, 103)

Froben had asked Erasmus to put a rush on a Greek copy of the New Testament. Erasmus was given an extremely short notice to get done, in haste, what should have taken a couple of years at a minimum. With only a half dozen manuscripts (Byzantine), with just one being moderately old and only slightly reliable. Erasmus went to work with none of the manuscripts containing the entire New Testament, Moreover, some verses were not even in this handful of manuscripts. Therefore, Erasmus had to actually translate the verses that had initially been translated from Greek into Latin back into Greek. There is no manuscript out of the 5,836+ that we have that contain this part of the Textus Receptus.

Martin Luther would use Erasmus' 1519 edition for his German translation, and William Tyndale would use the 1522 edition for his English translation. Erasmus' editions were also the foundation for later Greek editions of the New Testament by others. Among them were the four published by Robert Estienne (Stephanus, 1503-59). The third of these, published by Stephanus in 1550, became the Textus Receptus or Received Text of Britain and the basis for the King James Version. This took place through Theodore de Beza (1519-1605), whose work was based on the corrupted third and fourth editions of the Erasmian text. Beza would produce nine editions of the Greek text, four being independent (1565, 1589, 1588-9, 1598), and the other five smaller reprints. It would be two of Beza's editions, that of 1589 and 1598, which would become the English Received Text.

Beza's Greek edition of the New Testament did not even differ as much as might be expected from those of Erasmus. Why do I say, as might be expected? Beza was a friend of the Protestant reformer, John Calvin, succeeding him at Geneva, and was also a well-known classical and biblical scholar. In addition, Beza possessed two important Greek manuscripts of the fourth and fifth century, the **D** and **D**P(also known as **D**[2]), the former of which contains most of the Gospels and Acts as well as a fragment of 3 John, and the latter containing the Pauline epistles. The Dutch Elzevir editions followed next, which were virtually identical to those of the Erasmian-influenced Beza text. It was in the second of seven of these, published in 1633, that there appeared the statement in the preface (in

Latin): "You therefore now have the text accepted by everybody, in which we give nothing changed or corrupted." On the continent, this edition became the Textus Receptus or the Received Text. It seems that this success was in no small way due to the beauty and useful size of the Elzevir editions.

Why should this brief history of our Greek New Testament be so important to us? How can our knowing that Erasmus created the first printed master Greek text with chiefly two corrupt twelfth-century manuscripts help us today, some 500 years after 1516? The reason that it is important to us is because of the impact Erasmus' master Greek text had.

The fact that Erasmus was terribly rushed resulted in a Greek text that contained hundreds of typographical errors alone.[38] Textual scholar Scrivener once stated: '[It] is in that respect the most faulty book I know' (Scrivener 1894, 185). This comment did not even take into consideration the blatant interpolations into the text that were not part of the original. Sir Frederic Kenyon made this observation about the Textus Receptus, "The result is that the text accepted in the sixteenth and seventeenth centuries, to which we have clung from a natural reluctance to change the words which we have learnt as those of the Word of God, is in truth full of inaccuracies, many of which can be corrected with absolute certainty from the vastly wider information which is at our disposal today."[39] Erasmus was not oblivious to the typographical errors, which were corrected in a good many later editions. This did not include the textual errors. It was his second edition of 1519 that was used by Martin Luther in his German translation and William Tyndale's English translation.

The Restoration Period Reiterated for Emphasis

For the next 250 years, until 1881, textual scholarship was enslaved to the Erasmian-oriented Received Text. As these textual scholars[40] became familiar with older and more accurate manuscripts and observed the flaws in the Received Text, instead of changing the text, they would publish their findings in introductions, margins, and footnotes of their editions. In 1734,

---

[38] In fact, his copy of Revelation being incomplete, Erasmus simply retranslated the missing verses from the Latin Vulgate back into Greek.

[39] Frederic G. Kenyon Sr., Our Bible and the Ancient Manuscripts: Being a History of the Text and Its Translations (London: Eyre & Spottiswood, 1896), 162.

[40] Brian Walton (1600-61), Dr. John Fell (1625-86), John Mill 1645-1707), Dr. Edward Wells (1667-1727, Richard Bentley (1662-1742), John Albert Bengel (1687-1752), Johann Jacob Wettstein (1693-1754), Johann Salomo Semler (1725-91), William Bowyer Jr. (1699-1777), Edward Harwood (1729-94), and Isaiah Thomas Jr. (1749-1831)

J. A. Bengel of Tübingen, Germany, made an apology for again printing the Received Text, doing so only "because he could not publish a text of his own. Neither the publisher nor the public would have stood for it," he complained. (Robertson 1925, 25)

The first one to break free from this enslavement to the Textus Receptus, in the text itself, was Bible scholar J. J. Griesbach (1745-1812). His principal edition comes to us in three volumes, the first in Halle in 1775-7, the second in Halle and London in 1796-1806, and the third at Leipzig in 1803-7. However, Griesbach did not fully break from the Textus Receptus. Nevertheless, Griesbach is the real starting point in the development of classifying the manuscripts into families, setting down principles and rules for establishing the original reading, and using symbols to indicate the degree of certainty as to its being the original reading. We will examine his contributions in more detail below.

Karl Lachmann (1793-1851) was the first scholar fully to get out from under the influence of the Textus Receptus. He was a professor of ancient classical languages at Berlin University. In 1831, he published his edition of the Greek New Testament without any regard to the Textus Receptus. As Samuel MacAuley Jackson expressed it: Lachmann "was the first to found a text wholly on ancient evidence; and his editions, to which his eminent reputation as a critic gave wide currency, especially in Germany, did much toward breaking down the superstitious reverence for the textus receptus." Bruce Metzger had harsh words for the era of the Textus Receptus as well:

> So superstitious has been the reverence accorded the Textus Receptus that in some cases attempts to criticize it or emend it have been regarded as akin to sacrilege. Yet its textual basis is essentially a handful of late and haphazardly collected minuscule manuscripts, and in a dozen passages its reading is supported by no known Greek witnesses. (B. M. Metzger 1964, 1968, 1992, 106)

Subsequent to Lachmann came Friedrich Constantine von Tischendorf (1815-74), best known for his discovery of the famed fourth-century Codex Sinaiticus manuscript, the only Greek uncial manuscript containing the complete Greek New Testament. Tischendorf went further than any other textual scholar to edit and made accessible the evidence contained in leading as well as less important uncial manuscripts. Throughout the time that Tischendorf was making his valuable contributions to the field of textual criticism in Germany, another great scholar, Samuel Prideaux Tregelles (1813-75) in England made other valued contributions. Among them, he was able to establish his concept of "Comparative Criticism." That is, the age of a text, such as Vaticanus 1209, may not necessarily be that of its manuscript (i.e. the material upon which the text was written), which was copied in 350 C.E., since the text may be a faithful copy of an earlier text, like the second-century P[75]. Both Tischendorf and Tregelles were determined defenders of divine inspiration of the Scriptures, which likely had much to do with the productivity of their labors. If you take an opportunity to read about the lengths to which Tischendorf went in his discovery of Codex Sinaiticus, you will be moved by his steadfastness and love for God's Word.

The Climax of the Restored Text

The critical text of Westcott and Hort of 1881 has been commended by leading textual scholars over the last one hundred and forty years, and still stands as the standard. Numerous additional critical editions of the Greek text came after Westcott and Hort: Richard F. Weymouth (1886), Bernhard Weiss (1894–1900); the British and Foreign Bible Society (1904, 1958), Alexander Souter (1910), Hermann von Soden (1911–1913); and Eberhard Nestle's Greek text, *Novum Testamentum Graece*, published in 1898 by the Württemberg Bible Society, Stuttgart, Germany. The Nestle in twelve editions (1898–1923) to subsequently be taken over by his son, Erwin Nestle (13th–20th editions, 1927–1950), followed by Kurt Aland (21st–25th editions, 1952–1963), and lastly, it was coedited by Kurt Aland and Barbara Aland (26th–27th editions, 1979–1993).

Many of the above scholars gave their entire lives to God and the Greek text. Each of these could have an entire book devoted to them and their work alone. The amount of work they accomplished before the era of computers is nothing short of astonishing. Rightly, the preceding history should serve to strengthen our faith in the authenticity and general integrity of the Greek New Testament. Unlike Bart D. Ehrman, men like Sir Frederic Kenyon have been moved to say that the books of the Greek New Testament have "come down to us substantially as they were written." And all this is especially true of the critical scholarship of the almost two hundred years since the days of Karl Lachmann, due to which all today can feel certain that what they hold in their hands is a mirror reflection of the Word of God that was penned in twenty-seven books, some two thousand years ago.

Even though dozens of others had given their lives to the restoration of the Greek New Testament text, the pinnacle of those efforts came in the late 19th century with B. F. Westcott and F. J. A. Hort, who produced a restored text in 1881 that has been widely accepted. Westcott and Hort carried out their work so meticulously and thoroughly, possessing such knowledge insight, and skill that all textual scholars since then has been working in reaction to their work. This restored text of Westcott and Hort has been the basis for almost all modern-day translations. On this Metzger writes,

> Subsequently other critical editions appeared, including those prepared by Constantin von Tischendorf, whose eighth edition (1869–72) remains a monumental thesaurus of variant readings, and the influential edition prepared by two Cambridge scholars, B. F. Westcott and F. J. A. Hort (1881). **It is the latter edition that was taken as the basis for the present United Bible Societies' edition.** During the twentieth century, with the discovery of several New Testament manuscripts much older than any that had hitherto been available, it has become possible to produce editions of the New Testament that approximate ever more closely to what is regarded as the wording of the original documents.[41] (Bold mine)

Some Verses That Should Not Have Ever Been

Matthew 17:21 King James Version (KJV)	**Matthew 17:21** Updated American Standard Version (UASV)
[21] Howbeit this kind goeth not out but by prayer and fasting.	[21] ——[196]

Many later Greek manuscripts add vs 21, scribes making it agree with Mark 9:29, [But this kind does not go out except by prayer and fasting.] However, the earliest, weightiest, and diverse manuscripts ℵ* B Θ 0281 33 892* it^e Sy^c.s cop^sa WHNU does not contain vs 21.

Matthew 18:11 King James Version (KJV)	**Matthew 18:11** Updated American Standard Version (UASV)
[11] For the Son of man is come to save that which was lost.	[11] ——[202]

---

[41] Bruce Manning Metzger, United Bible Societies, *A Textual Commentary on the Greek New Testament, Second Edition a Companion Volume to the United Bible Societies' Greek New Testament (4th Rev. Ed.)* (London; New York: United Bible Societies, 1994), xxiv.

The earliest and most trusted two manuscripts (א B) do not include variant 1 or variant 2. Also excluding these variants is L* Θ* f¹. 33 itᵉ syrˢ copˢᵃ Origen as well. Multiple later manuscripts (D L W Θᶜ 078 Maj syrᶜˑᵖ) ad variant 1: "For the Son of Man has come to save that which was lost." Several other manuscripts (Lᵐᵍ 892ᶜ itᶜ syrʰ) would expand upon this reading in variant 2: "For the Son of Man came to seek and to save the lost." Based on their not being in the most important and trusted witnesses and diverse witnesses (Alexandrian, Egyptian, Antiochian), clearly, variant 1 and variant 2 are interpolations (spurious) were not part of the original. It seems that the copyists inserted this verse in the text to create some sort of bridge between Matthew 18:10 and 18:12, so they borrowed it from Luke 19:10, which is not even parallel to this one. In all likelihood, the shorter variant came first, and a later copyist expanded upon it with the longer variant 2, bringing it to the point where it corresponds exactly with Luke 19:10.

Matthew 23:14 King James Version (KJV)	Matthew 23:14 Updated American Standard Version (UASV)
¹⁴ Woe unto you, scribes and Pharisees, hypocrites! for ye devour widows' houses, and for a pretence make long prayer: therefore ye shall receive the greater damnation.	¹⁴ —[247]

This verse was taken from Mark 12:40 or Luke 20:47 and inserted **before** verse 13 of Matthew Chapter 24 in the *Majority Text* (W 0102 0107 it syrʰˑᵖ) but **after** verse 13 in the *Textus Receptus* (f¹³ it syrᶜ). It was not in the original text of Matthew per it not being in the early weighty documentary witnesses against the reading from the Alexandrian and Western text types. (א B D L Z Θ f¹ 33 it·ᵉ syrˢ copˢᵃ) This type of harmonization of the gospels was common after the fourth century CE and is characteristic of the Byzantine text-type. Both the KJV and the NKJV part company with the Textus Receptus and instead went with the Majority Text when they placed the verse after verse 13. Many modern-day translations cite the verse in a footnote out of respect for its long history in the English Bible. The HCSB and the NASB take it to the next level out of reverence for the KJV and the NKJV readers, so they place this interpolation right in the main text within square brackets with footnotes that read, "Other mss omit bracketed text" and "This v not found in early mss" respectively. However, it should be noted that the 2017 CSB removed this spurious verse from the main text. The HCSB and the NASB are not helping their readers by clinging to a translation that is based on corrupt, inferior manuscripts support.

Mark 7:16 King James Version (KJV)	Mark 7:16 Updated American Standard Version (UASV)
16 If any man have ears to hear, let him hear.	16 ——[41]

WH NU אּ B L Δ * 0274 al omit; A D W Θ f¹.¹³ 33 Maj, "If anyone has ears to hear, let him hear." The scribe clearly added this verse from 4:9 or 4:23, as it is nearly identical, possibly seeking to provide an ending for a short pericope.

Mark 9:44, 46 King James Version (KJV)	Mark 9:44, 46 Updated American Standard Version (UASV)
44 Where their worm dieth not, and the fire is not quenched. 46 Where their worm dieth not, and the fire is not quenched.	44 ——[53] 46 ——[55]

WH NU אּ B C L W ΔΨ 0274 f¹ 28 565 itᵏ syrˢ cop omit; A D Θ f¹³ Maj, "where their worm does not die and the fire is not quenched." This verse is identical to verse 48 and is missing from the earliest and best manuscripts, as well as several text types. It is an interpolation.

WH NU אּ B C L W ΔΨ 0274 f¹ 28 565 itᵏ syrˢ cop omit; A D Θ f¹³ Maj, "where their worm does not die and the fire is not quenched." This verse is identical to verse 48 and is missing from the earliest and best manuscripts, as well as several text types. It is an interpolation.

Mark 11:26 King James Version (KJV)	Mark 11:26 Updated American Standard Version (UASV)
26 But if ye do not forgive, neither will your Father which is in heaven forgive your trespasses.	26 ——[63]

Many later Greek manuscripts added vs 26, as the scribes were expanding on verse 25, inserting the words from Matt. 6:15 making it agree with its parallel account. [But if you do not forgive, neither will your Father who is in the heavens forgive your trespasses.] However, the omission has much stronger manuscript support: א B L W Δ Ψ 565 700 syr^s WH NU omit vs 26.

Mark 15:28 King James Version (KJV)	Mark 15:28 Updated American Standard Version (UASV)
28 And the scripture was fulfilled, which saith, And he was numbered with the transgressors.	28 ——[93]

WH NU omit verse, which is supported by the earliest and best manuscripts א A B C D Ψ it^k syr^s cop^{sa}. A variant/TR add verse Και επληρωθη η γραφη η λεγουσα· και μετα ανομων ελογισθη "And the Scripture was fulfilled that says, 'He was counted among the lawless,'" which is supported by L Θ 083 0250 f^{1,13} Maj syr^{h,p}.

Luke 17:36 King James Version (KJV)	Luke 17:36 Updated American Standard Version (UASV)
36 Two men shall be in the field; the one shall be taken, and the other left.	36—[134]

The earliest and most reliable manuscripts (P⁷⁵ א A B L W Δ Θ Ψ f¹ 33 cop^{·bo}) does not contain 17:36, while later manuscripts (D f 700 it syr) does contain verse 36, "Two men will be in the field; one will be taken and the other will be left." This is likely a scribal interpolation taken from Matthew 24:40. This verse is missing from Tyndale's version (1534) and the Geneva Bible (1557). Even the King James Version translators had their doubts about 17:36, as it reads in the original 1611 edition and a sidenote in good quality editions today, "This 36th verse is wanting in most of the Greek copies."

John 5:3b-4 King James Version (KJV)	John 5:3b-4 Updated American Standard Version (UASV)
3 In these lay a great multitude of impotent folk, of blind, halt, withered, waiting for the moving of the water. 4 For an angel went down at a certain season into the pool, and troubled the water: whosoever	3 In these lay a multitude of sick ones, blind, lame, and paralyzed. 4—[29]

then first after the troubling of the water stepped in was made whole of whatsoever disease he had.	

The earliest and best witnesses (P66 P75 ℵ B C D L T Ws 33 579 1241 it syc co) do not have John 5:3b-4 in their exemplar; Other later witnesses (Ac C3 D K Ws Γ Δ Θ Ψ 078 f1.13 33. 565. 579. 700. 892. 1241. 1424 Maj lat syp.h bopt) did contain: "waiting for the moving of the water. 4 For an angel of the Lord would come down at certain seasons into the pool and stirred the water. Whoever went in first after the stirring of the water was healed of whatever disease he had." This interpolation was added by later scribes to explain the sick man's answer in verses 7 where he describes 'the water being stirred up.'

Acts 8:37 King James Version (KJV)	Acts 8:37 Updated American Standard Version (UASV)
37 And Philip said, If thou believest with all thine heart, thou mayest. And he answered and said, I believe that Jesus Christ is the Son of God.	37—[22]

The earliest and best Greek manuscripts (P45. 74 ℵ A B C) as well as 33 81 614 vg syrp.h copsa.bo eth Chrysostom Ambrose do not contain vs 37, while other manuscripts 4mg (E 1739 it syrh** Irenaeus Cyprian) contain, And Philip said, "If you believe with all your heart, you may." And he replied, "I believe that Jesus Christ is the Son of God." If this were apart of the original, there is no good reason why it would be missing in so many early witnesses and versions. This is a classic example of a scribe taking liberties with the text by answering the Eunuch's question ("Look! Water! What prevents me from being baptized?") with ancient Christian baptismal practices from a later age.

Acts 15:34 King James Version (KJV)	Acts 15:34 Updated American Standard Version (UASV)
34 Notwithstanding it pleased Silas to abide there still.	34—[128]

Verse 34 is not contained in the earliest and diverse manuscripts (P74 ℵ A B E Ψ Maj syrp copbo), while vs 34 is contained in two different forms in other manuscripts (C 33 614 1739 syr** copsa) "But it seemed good to Silas to remain there" and (P[127vid] D it·ʷ) "But it seemed good to Silas to remain with them, so Judas traveled alone." The scribes likely incorporated a gloss from the margin that was trying to rationalize why Silas just happened to be there in verse 40 for the apostle Paul to choose him as a traveling companion. The only problem is that the interpolation of vs 34 contradicts vs 33.

Acts 24:6b–8a King James Version (KJV)	Acts 24:6b–8a Updated American Standard Version (UASV)
[6] Who also hath gone about to profane the temple: whom we took, and would have judged according to our law. [7] But the chief captain Lysias came upon us, and with great violence took him away out of our hands, [8] Commanding his accusers to come unto thee: by examining of whom thyself mayest take knowledge of all these things, whereof we accuse him.	[6] He even tried to desecrate the temple, but we seized him. [7] — —[254] [8] When you examine him yourself, you will find out about all these things of which we are accusing him."

P[74] ℵ A B H L P 049 cop omit the following from vss 6-8, which read, according to (E) Ψ Maj 33 614 1739 it (syr): "We wanted to judge him according to our own Law. [7] But Lysias the commander came along, and with much violence took him out of our hands, [8] ordering his accusers to come before you." The earliest and most reliable manuscripts have the shorter reading. The interpolation is a classic example of a scribe trying to fill in what he perceives to be gaps in the text.

Acts 28:29 King James Version (KJV)	Acts 28:29 Updated American Standard Version (UASV)
[29] And when he had said these words, the Jews departed, and had great reasoning among themselves.	[29]—[287]

The earliest and best Greek manuscripts (P[74] ℵ A B E Ψ 048 33 1739 syr[p] cop) do not contain vs 29, while is later less trusted manuscripts (Maj it syr[h**]) that contain Acts 28:29, "When he had spoken these words, the

Jews departed, having a great dispute among themselves." This is another example of later scribes seeking to fill in the narrative where they perceive there is a gap in the account.

Romans 16:24 King James Version (KJV)	Romans 16:24 Updated American Standard Version (UASV)
24 The grace of our Lord Jesus Christ be with you all. Amen.	24 ——[112]

The earliest and best manuscripts (P46 P61 א A B C 1739 It^b cop) do not contain vs 24, while later witnesses (D Ψ Maj syr^h) contain 16:24, "The grace of our Lord Jesus Christ be with you all. Amen," with F G omitting Ιησου Χριστου [Jesus Christ]. This verse is the same as the end of vs 20. All modern translations do not include this verse because of the superior testimony against it.

1 John 5:7-8 King James Version (KJV)	1 John 5:7-8 Updated American Standard Version (UASV)
7 For there are three that bear record in heaven, the Father, the Word, and the Holy Ghost: and these three are one. 8 And there are three that bear witness in earth, the Spirit, and the water, and the blood: and these three agree in one.	7 For there are three that testify:[16] 8 the Spirit and the water and the blood; and the three are in agreement.

The earliest and best manuscripts (א A B (Ψ) Maj syr cop arm eth it) do not contain this spurious interpolation. Only eight late Greek manuscripts add "... in heaven, the Father, the Word, and the Holy Spirit, and these three are one. 8 And there are three that testify on earth, the Spirit." If this passage had been in the original, there is no good reason why it would have been removed either accidentally or intentionally. None of the Greek church fathers quote this passage, which they certainly would have during the Trinitarian controversy. (Sabellian and Arian). This interpolation is not in any of the ancient versions, such as Syriac, Coptic, Armenian, Ethiopic, Arabic, Slavonic, and the Old Latin in its early form, or Jerome's Latin Vulgate. Intrinsically, the interpolation "makes an awkward break in the sense" as Metzger points out.

Some other verses that contain interpolations (italics is the spurious portion) are **Matthew 20:16 (b) KJV:** [16] ... *for many be called, but few chosen.* **Mark 6:11 (b) KJV:** [11] And whosoever shall not receive you, nor hear you, when ye depart thence, shake off the dust under your feet, for a testimony against them: *Verily I say unto you, it shall be more tolerable for Sodom and Gomorrah in the Day of Judgement, than for that city.* [12] And they went out, and preached ... **Luke 4:8 (b) KJV:** [8] And Jesus answered and said unto to him [the Devil], "*Get thee behind me, Satan, for* it is written, ..." **Luke 23:17 KJV:** *For of necessity he must release one unto them at the feast.* **Acts 9:5-6 KJV:** [5] And he [Paul] said, 'Who art thou Lord?' and the Lord said, 'I am Jesus whom thou persecutest. *It is hard for thee to kick against the pricks.'* [6] *And he, trembling and astonished, said, 'Lord, what wilt thou have me to do?' And the Lord said unto him,* 'Arise, and go into the city, and it shall be told thee what thou must do.'

Translation Chart from Wikipedia

O = omitted in main text.

B = bracketed in the main text – The translation team and most biblical scholars today believe were not part of the original text. However, these texts have been retained in brackets in the NASB and the Holman CSB.[140]

F = omission noted in the footnote.

Passage	NIV	NASB	NKJV	NRSV	ESV	HCSB	NET	NLT	WEB
Bible Translations									
Matthew 9:34									
Matthew 12:47				F	F	F		F	
Matthew 17:21	F	B	F	O	F	B	O	F	

Reference								
Matthew 18:11	F	B	F	O	F	B	O	O
Matthew 21:44			F	F		B		F
Matthew 23:14	F	B	F	O	F	B	O	O
Mark 7:16	F	B	F	O	F	B	O	O
Mark 9:44	F	B	F	O	F	B	O	O
Mark 9:46	F	B	F	O	F	B	O	O
Mark 11:26	F	B	F	O	F	B	O	O
Mark 15:28	F	B	F	O	F	B	O	O
Mark 16:9–20	B	B	F	F	B	B	B	
Luke 17:36	F	B	F	O	F	B	O	O	F
Luke 22:20					F		F	
Luke 22:43		B	F	F		B	B	F
Luke 22:44		B	F	F		B	B	F
Luke 23:17	F	B	F	O	F	B	O	O
Luke 24:12								
Luke 24:40				F				

John 5:4	F	B	F	O	F	B	O	O	
John 7:53–8:11		B	F	F	B	B	B		
Acts 8:37	F	B	F	F	F	B	O	O	F
Acts 15:34	F	B	F	O	F	O	O	O	F
Acts 24:7	F	B	F	O	F	B	O	O	F
Acts 28:29	F	B	F	O	F	B	O	O	
Romans 16:24	F	B	F	O	F	B	O	O	

As was mentioned above, some scribes have added a sentence or even an entire verse from elsewhere to another part of the manuscript he was copying. This is clearly made evident in Mark 9:43-48. In the above Bible translations, you can see that verses 44 and 46 are omitted in the main text with the omission noted in the footnote. The only exception in the NASB and the HCSB, which bracketed 44 and 46 in the main text. These translation committees and most biblical scholars today believe verses 44 and 46 were not part of the original text. It could be the translation committees are clinging to the King James Version readers. The text of verses 44 and 46 reads, "where their worm does not die, and the fire is not quenched," the same as in verse 48.

Mark 9:44: WH NU א B C L W ΔΨ 0274 f¹ 28 565 itᵏ syrˢ cop omit; A D Θ f¹³ Maj, "where their worm does not die and the fire is not quenched." This verse is identical to verse 48 and is missing from the earliest and best manuscripts, as well as several text types. It is an interpolation.

Mark 9:46: WH NU א B C L W ΔΨ 0274 f¹ 28 565 itᵏ syrˢ cop omit; A D Θ f¹³ Maj, "where their worm does not die and the fire is not quenched." This verse is identical to verse 48 and is missing from the earliest and best manuscripts, as well as several text types. It is an interpolation.

Clearly, as the evidence suggests a scribe or scribes simply repeated verse 48. This could have been intentional or unintentional. Therefore, when modern translations remove verse 44 and 46; they are not removing part of God's Word because (1) it was never a part of God's Word in the first place and (2) the same sentence is right there in verse 48 of the same account. However, what are these translations accomplishing by removing these two spurious interpolations? The text is being restored to what Mark had been inspired to write.

Looking again at our example verse above, we note that there are other cases where the verses come not from the same book but from another book of the Bible. There are generally footnotes that help the reader to see this but often, the translations do not give the reader enough information so he or she can fully understand. If you compare your King James Version with the modern translations, you will discover that the verse that has been omitted, it is merely a verse repeated from another place in that book or another Bible book. If we look at Romans 16:24 again, we will see that the earliest and best manuscripts (P^{46} P^{61} א A B C 1739 It^b cop) do not contain vs 24, while later witnesses (D Ψ Maj syr^h) contain 16:24, "The grace of our Lord Jesus Christ be with you all. Amen," with F G omitting Ιησου Χριστου [Jesus Christ]. This verse is the same as the end of vs 20. All modern translations do not include this verse because of the superior testimony against it. When we compare 16:24 with 16:20 and the closing passages in almost any of the books written by the apostle Paul, we discover that at Romans 16:24, some scribe plainly added a closing expression that is identical to or very similar to the conclusion in almost all of Paul's books.

Trusting the Greek New Testament

As we have looked at a few verses that obviously were not part of the original inspired text that the author penned, this should not leave us doubting the trustworthiness of God's Word. We should not that 90% of the Hebrew Old Testament Text is without significant variation and 93% of the Greek New Testament Text is without significant variation. We have the work of hundreds of textual scholars from the days of Desiderius Erasmus, who have given their entire lives to the restoration of the Greek New Testament. Therefore, textual scholars only need to focus their attention on this very small 07% of significant textual variants. These variants that have been corrected have not undermined the Word of God, rather they highlight and stress the fact that God has preserved his Word through restoration.

Chapter 7 deals with providing insights into the King James Version that most readers are not aware. What do most readers of the King James Bible not know about the translation that they use?

CHAPTER 18 Do You Really Know the King James Version?

Edward D. Andrews

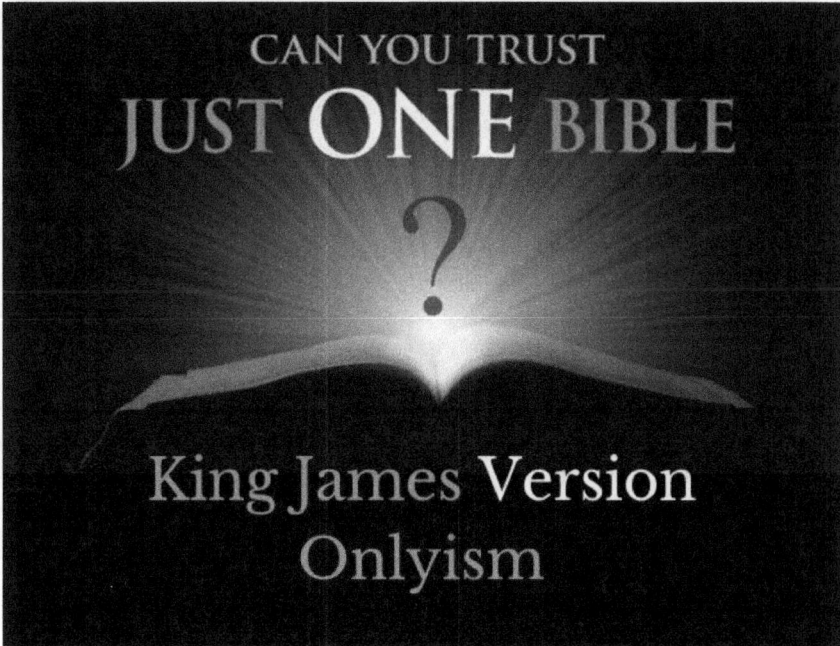

CAN YOU TRUST
JUST ONE BIBLE
?
King James Version
Onlyism

"**Willful blindness** (sometimes called ignorance of law, willful ignorance or contrived ignorance or Nelsonian knowledge) is a term used in law to describe a situation in which a person seeks to avoid civil or criminal liability for a wrongful act by intentionally keeping himself or herself unaware of facts that would render him or her liable."[42] This is the case with many of the King James Version readers, who are known as the King James Version Only. The King James Version Only followers, as we might call them, they are willfully blind, in that they intentionally keep themselves and others unaware of facts from how the Bible came down to us from the original Hebrew Old Testament and Greek New Testament manuscripts, to the copyists of these books of the Bible, to the early version, and finally the translations that would enable them to be fully informed.

---

[42] Criminal Law – Cases and Materials, 7th ed. 2012, Wolters Kluwer Law & Business; John Kaplan, Robert Weisberg, Guyora Binder, - Wikipedia.

For example, you have the so-called Pastor and Bible Teacher Mark Wright[43] of an online Bible School. Richling states that the King James Bible is not "the final authority," as most King James Only believers commonly proffer. Rather, Wright goes on to say, "that is a lie that is not true, the King James Bible is all authority. You see if it is the final authorities leading up to it and that is simply not the case. There is no authority leading up to the Word of God and the Word of God ends up being the final authority. No, the King James Bible is all authority. That's what God says in his book." This would seem to suggest that even the inspired authors of God's Word are not the true authority but only the King Kames Bible. While Mark Wright is an extreme example, going beyond the King James Only group, they are not far behind.

What most of these King James Only readers and those who simply prefer the King James Bible do not know about this translation. Many readers of the King James Bible argue most about other translations that supposedly changed the Bible by taking things out of the Bible. First, it is not removing words, phrases, sentences, and whole verses from the Bible, if they were never in the original to start with but were added later by copyists who took intentional liberties with the text or accidentally altered the original language texts. Those who argue that the modern translations of the Bible are guilty of changing the Bible (what they mean changing the King James Version), they do not know that the King James Version has already been changed in thousands of ways?

A common joke among those who are aware of how the Bible came down to us is the attempt by King James Version Only readers in their defense of the King James Bible, they often say, "If the Authorized Version was good enough for St. Paul, it is good enough for me." First, we would note that Paul lived 1,500 years before the King James Bible came into existence and the English language itself was not even in existence in Paul's day. The truth is the King James version is used by more of the English-speaking world than any other single translation. As we have shown, it is so esteemed that many persons revere, even worship it as the only true Bible.

These countless Millions who use the King James version believe that it is satanic or rather that it is Satan who is responsible with the modern-day translations keep rolling off the presses. The KJVO pastors, priests, and ministers are the ones, who propagate this line. The irony is that the average churchgoer, as well as most church leadership, has no idea of the history of the King James Version itself let along all other aspects of God's Word: such

---

[43] The name has been changed

as the Old Testament and New Testament manuscripts, the early versions, the translations before the King James Version or anything that took place after 1611. They do not even know what illuminating document is probably missing from their own copies of the King James Bible. Sadly, they do not even know their own King James Bible.

God himself is the author of the sixty-six books that we call the Bible, wherein he used 40+ human authors, as he moved them along by the Holy Spirit. The original manuscripts by these inspired authors were inerrant, infallible, without error. This is not true of the copyist thereafter or the translators. What is the purpose of Bible translation? It is to take the thoughts of God, originally written in Hebrew, Aramaic, and Greek, and put them into the current languages of today, such as English. It was for this reason that the Tyndale, Coverdale, the Great Bible, the Geneva Bible, the Bishop's Bible and the King James Version came into existence. That latter was in 1611.

Early English Bible History

Earlier we learned how many English translations of the Bible had come into being. There was the first handwritten translation by **John Wycliffe** in 1380. **Martin Luther** would translate the New Testament into German for the first time from the corrupt 1516 Greek-Latin New Testament of **Desiderius Erasmus** and publish it in September of 1522. **William Tyndale** wanted to use the same 1516 Erasmus text (Textus Receptus) as a source to translate and print the first New Testament into English for the first time in history. Tyndale came to Luther's in Germany in 1525, and by the end of the year, he had translated the New Testament into English. For his efforts, Tyndale was incarcerated for almost one and half years before he was strangled and burned at the stake in 1536. **Miles Coverdale** finished his translation work the Old Testament, and in 1535 he printed the first complete Bible in the English language. Thus, the first complete English Bible was printed on October 4, 1535, and became known as the Coverdale Bible. Just three years later in 1539 King Henry funded the printing of an English Bible known as the **Great Bible**. Then, we had the Geneva Bible of 1560 and the Bishops' Bible of 1568.

Some 36 years later, King James I started the translation project that would bring us the King James Version. It would not be a translation from the Original but rather it would be a revision of the versions then in use. This is evident from the instructions given by King James to the translators. They were to use the Bishop's Bible with the instruction to not deviate from it as little as possible. If Tyndale's, Matthew's, Coverdale's, Whitchurch's, and the Geneva Bible agreed over and against the Bishop's Bible, it was to be the preferred reading. In 1611, a new translation emerged on the scenes, basically ended up being the Tyndale-Coverdale text and some improved alterations from the KJV translators themselves. These improvements focused particularly on the choice of words and enrichment of the rhythmic quality of the text. The result was a version that was superior to its predecessors as to the accuracy of translation and the refinement of literary style. Were the church leaders and churchgoers of 1611 rejoicing over the fact that they had a superior, more accurate translation of God's Word, giving them God's thoughts more correctly than all of the numerous previous English translations?

The Irony of It All

Even before the publication of this new and improved translation, the King James Version, was final, it faced opposition. Why? The church leaders and the churchgoers were quite familiar with and happy with the English translations that they had been using, feeling as though they already had a trusted translation of God's thoughts. The people preferred to keep the translations that they were already familiar with and trusted. These church leaders and churchgoers lost sight of the whole purpose of the Bible itself. Paul tells us at 2 Timothy 3:16-17, "All Scripture is inspired by God and profitable for teaching, for reproof, for correction, for training in righteousness; so that the man of God may be fully competent, equipped for every good work." Certainly, being familiar with, trusting and preferring the Geneva Bible is not keeping in mind the purpose of God's Word and the purpose of translating in the first place. The irony is that here we are defending the improved translation work of the King James Version over its predecessors, previous English translations, from Bible readers of 1611 that wanted to retain a translation (e.g., the Geneva Bible) that they preferred because it was familiar to them; thus, they trusted it.

From almost every quarter the King James Bible was being hammered with opposition. Criticism was frequently severe. Hugh Broughton (1549 – 1612) was an English scholar of Hebrew and a theologian of the day, who wrote King James, where he criticized the new translation unsparingly, saying that he "would rather be torn asunder by wild horses than allow such a version to be imposed on the church."[44] The King James Version translators were unaware that the people of 1611 preferred to keep the translations that they had already grown familiar with, but they were well

---

[44] Robert Burns Wallace, *An Introduction to the Bible as Literature* (London, England, UK: Westminster Press, 1929), 299.

aware that their translation work had unleashed a storm. They attempted to calm the waters by writing a "Preface of the Translators" to explain why the King James Version had been made.

However, most King James Versions being printed today, many decent decades really, though they contain a lengthy dedication to King James, they omit from the usual printings the "Preface of the Translators." If they retained this preface, the modern King James Version reader would have a better understanding of the purpose of the revision. First, the reader would be aware that the King James Version was an improved revision of other earlier English translations. Second, the reader would learn that opposition to a revised translation is to be expected because people are familiar with their current trusted translation that they feel to be the most accurate. Third, the reader would be more receptive to the current translations that they make the exact same argument about say, "we do not want to use your revisions (RV 1881, ASV 1902, RSV 1952, NRSV 1989, NASB 1995, ESV 2001, UASV, 2018), as we have the one true translation that we trust and know."

In part the "Preface of the Translators" says:

> Many mens mouths haue bene open a good while (and yet are not stopped) with speeches about the Translation so long in hand . . . : and aske what may be the reason, what the necessitie of the employment.[45] [Many men's mouths have been open a good while (and yet are not stopped) with speeches about the Translation so long in hand . . . : and asked what may be the reason, what the necessity of the employment.]

Again, the King James Version reader would learn that the *King James Version* was a revision of earlier English Translations made with a modest hope of improvement and they had no thought of finality:

> Truly (good Christian Reader) wee neuer thought from the beginning, that we should neede to make a new Translation, nor yet to make of a bad one a good one, . . . but to make a good one better, or out of many good ones, one principall good one, not justly to be excepted against; that hath bene our indeauour, that our marke.[46] [Truly (good Christian Reader) we never thought from the beginning, that we should need to make a new Translation, nor yet to make of a bad one a good one, . . . but

---

[45] Gordon Campbell, *The Holy Bible: King James Version, Quatercentenary Edition* (Oxford, England, UK: Oxford University Press, 2010), xv.
[46] IBID.

to make a good one better, or out of many good ones, one principal good one, not justly to be excepted against; that has been our endeavor, that our mark.]

In his study on the King James Bible and its tradition, Alister McGrath writes: "A careful study of the way in which the King James Bible translates the Greek and Hebrew originals suggests that the translators felt obliged to: 1) Ensure that every word in the original was rendered by an English equivalent; 2) Make it clear when they added any words to make the sense clearer, or to lead to better English syntax. . . . 3) Follow the basic word order of the original wherever possible."[47]

Bruce M. Metzger writes, "The aim of the revisers is clearly stated in the preface. It was not to make 'a new translation, nor yet to make of a bad one a good one ... but to make a good one better, or out of many good ones one principal good one.' Although usually called a translation,' it is in fact merely a revision of the Bishops' Bible, as this itself was a revision of the Great Bible, and the Great Bible a revision of Coverdale and Tyndale. A great deal of the praise, therefore, that is given to it belongs to its predecessors. For the idiom and vocabulary, Tyndale deserves the greatest credit; for the melody and harmony, Coverdale;5 for scholarship and accuracy, the Geneva version."[48]

Leland Ryken observes, "within a few decades it supplanted the Geneva Bible as the dominant English version. Although the KJV eventually came to be known as the Authorized Version—the AV—it did not, in fact, receive the advantage of being officially sanctioned by either the king or the clerical hierarchy (even though the title page claimed that it was 'appointed to be read in Churches')."[49]

Changes to the King James Version

Today no one reads the *King James Version* in its original form of 1611. Many readers of the King James Version would be quite surprised to know of the many changes to the King James Bible throughout the centuries. There have been so many changes to the King James Version the Committee on Versions (1851-56) of the American Bible Society found 24,000 variations in six different editions of the King James Version! Metzger tells

---

[47] John Beekman and John Callow, *Translating the Word of God* (Grand Rapids, MI: Zondervan, 1974), 25.

[48] Bruce Metzger. Bible in Translation, The: Ancient and English Versions (pp. 76-77).

[49] Ryken, Leland. Understanding English Bible Translation: The Case for an Essentially Literal Approach (Kindle Locations 638-641). Crossway. Kindle Edition.

us that "the first printing of the version, as would be expected, contained some typographic errors-averaging about one in ten pages. In Exodus 14:10, three whole lines were repeated: "the children of Israel lift up their eyes, and beholde, the Egyptians marched after them, and they were sore afraid." A printer's error that has been perpetuated in editions of the KJV to the present time is "strain at a gnat" (Matt. 23:24) instead of "strain out a gnat." Of all the misprints that have disfigured various printings of the version, none has been so scandalous as the omission of the word "not" from the seventh commandment in an edition of 1631, which then read "Thou shalt commit adultery" (Exod. 20:14), for which the king's printers were fined three hundred pounds by Archbishop Laud."[50]

The argument from the King James reader, who refuses to even consider the updated, revised, far more accurate modern translations is that the Bible has been changed and they believe that the King James Version was perfect, some even thinking it was an inspired translation, the very inerrant, authoritative Word of God that has never been changed, error-free. Sadly, for these readers, the King James Version has already been changed many times and has thousands of errors, so their beliefs about the King James Version is extremely mistaken, lying on a crumbled foundation. In addition, why do the modern day King James Version readers not read the 1611 edition? Because the King James Version today, with its many corrections over the centuries is far easier to read. They are unknowingly not aware of the improvements to the King James Version. They would not want to read "fet" for "fetched," "sith" for "since" or "moe" for "more," as the edition of 1611 had it.

If these persons do not want it changed, then why do they use, instead of a copy of an edition of 1611, an edition that has been changed? They use a present-day edition of the King James Bible because it is far easier to read. They appreciate, perhaps unknowingly, the improvements the later editions have made. They do not like the odd spelling and punctuation of the 1611 edition; they do not want to read "fet" for "fetched," "sith" for "since" or "moe" for "more," as the edition of 1611 had it. Thus, improvement, when needed, is unknowingly appreciated, even by those who say they do not want modern translations because they have changed the Bible.

The English of the 1611 era is as such at Roman 6:1-7, "What shall we saye then? Shall we continue in synne that there maye be aboundaunce of grace? God forbyd. How shall we that are deed as touchynge synne live eny lenger therin? Remember ye not that all we which are baptysed in the

---

[50] Bruce Metzger. Bible in Translation, The: Ancient and English Versions (p. 78).

name of Iesu Christ are baptysed to dye with him? We are buryed with him by baptim for to dye that lykewyse as Christ was raysed vp from deeth by the glorye of the father: eve so we also shuld walke in a newe lyfe. For yf we be graft in deeth lyke vnto him: even so must we be in the resurreccio. This we must remeber that oure olde man is crucified with him also that the body of synne mygth vtterly be destroyed that hence forth we shuld not be servauntes of synne. For he that is deed ys iustified from synne. Wherfore yf we be deed with Christ we beleve that we shall live with him: 9 remembringe that Christ once raysed fro deeth dyeth no more. Deeth hath no moare power over him."

The vast number of improvements to the King James Version over the centuries is just a fraction of what is needed, which modern literal translations are providing to their readers by keeping pace with changing language. Therefore, they are making God's Word clear, understandable, alive.

The Sixteen Missing Verses Or The Sixteen Added Verses?

This is just some of the lengthier interpolations that the unaware propagate by saying that they are missing. **Interpolation:** the addition of spurious material to the text by a scribe. Philip Comfort glossary reads, "**Interpolation.** inserted new word or words that results in changing the original text."[51] These verses are not missing from the modern translations, they were not in the original text, as they were later additions to the Greek New Testament text by the copyist.

Matthew 17:21 King James Version (KJV)	Matthew 17:21 American Standard Version (ASV), Also ESV, LEB, CSB, UASV, others
[21] Howbeit this kind goeth not out but by prayer and fasting.	[21] _____

Matthew 17:21

The external evidence against including this verse is substantial, including ℵ* B (the two earliest manuscripts), 0281 (a seventh-century manuscript discovered at St. Catherine's Monastery in the late twentieth century), and early witnesses of Old Latin, Coptic, and Syriac. If the verse was originally part of Matthew's gospel, there is no good reason to explain

---

[51] Philip Comfort, *Encountering the Manuscripts: An Introduction to New Testament Paleography & Textual Criticism* (Nashville, TN: Broadman & Holman, 2005), 385.

why it was dropped from so many early and diverse witnesses. Thus, it is far more likely that this added verse was assimilated from Mark 9:29 in its long form, which has the additional words "and fasting." In fact, the same manuscripts ($\aleph^2$ C D L W f^1· Maj) that have the long form in Mark 9:29 have the additional verse here. Thus, a scribe took the full verse of Mark 9:29 as presented in his manuscript and inserted it here; most other manuscripts maintained this insertion in the transmission of the text. (The short form in Mark 9:29 appears in $\aleph$* B.) The verse is included in KJV and NKJV and excluded in all other modern versions except NASB and HCSB which include the verse in brackets.[52]

Matthew 18:11 King James Version (KJV)	Matthew 8:11 American Standard Version (ASV), Also ESV, LEB, CSB, UASV, others
[11] For the Son of man is come to save that which was lost.	11 _____

Matthew 18:11

The absence of this verse in several important and diverse witnesses attests to the fact that it was not part of the original text of Matthew. It was borrowed from Luke 19:10, a passage not at all parallel to this one. Most likely the addition first appeared in the shorter form (variant 1), and was later expanded to the longer form (variant 2), which concurs exactly with Luke 19:10. The manuscript L demonstrates all three phases: L* omits the verse; L has the shorter form of the addition, and L has the longer form.

Very likely this verse was inserted in Matt 18 to provide some sort of bridge between verses 10 and 12. In other words, a scribe perceived there was a semantic gap that needed filling. Luke 19:10 was used to introduce the illustration of a shepherd seeking out its lost sheep (the longer form also speaks of "seeking out," which makes the connection even clearer). However, the text must be read without the bridge that 18:11 provides. Verse 12 follows verse 10 in the original in that it provides yet another reason for why the "little ones who believe in Jesus" should not be despised: The shepherd is concerned for each and every sheep in the flock. In a flock of 100 sheep, if even one leaves, he will seek it out and find it.[53]

---

[52] Philip W. Comfort, *New Testament Text and Translation Commentary: Commentary on the Variant Readings of the Ancient New Testament Manuscripts and How They Relate to the Major English Translations* (Carol Stream, IL: Tyndale House Publishers, Inc., 2008), 51.

[53] IBID, 52–53.

Matthew 23:14 King James Version (KJV)	Matthew 23:14 American Standard Version (ASV), Also ESV, LEB, CSB, UASV, others
[14] Woe unto you, scribes and Pharisees, hypocrites! for ye devour widows' houses, and for a pretence make long prayer: therefore ye shall receive the greater damnation.	[14] ———

Matthew 23:14

This verse, not present in the earliest manuscripts and several other witnesses, was taken from Mark 12:40 or Luke 20:47 and inserted in later manuscripts either before or after 23:13. This kind of gospel harmonization became especially prevalent after the fourth century. It is noteworthy that KJV and NKJV did not follow TR in placing the verse before verse 13, but after it. The verse is noted in modern versions out of deference for its place in English Bible history. Undoubtedly, the HCSB includes the verse out of deference to its KJV- and NKJV-friendly readership, but this does not help these readers understand that KJV is based on inferior manuscript support.[54]

Mark 7:16 King James Version (KJV)	Mark 7:16 American Standard Version (ASV), Also ESV, LEB, CSB, UASV, others
[16] If any man have ears to hear, let him hear.	[16] ———

Mark 7:16

The WH NU reading has the earliest support among the manuscripts. The extra verse was added by scribes, borrowing it directly from 4:23 (see also 4:9) to provide an ending to an otherwise very short pericope, 7:14–15. This addition was included in TR and made popular by KJV, NKJV, NASB, NJB, and HCSB also include this extra verse.[55]

Mark 9:44 & 9:46 King James Version (KJV)	Mark 9:44 & 9:46 American Standard Version (ASV)), Also ESV, LEB, CSB, UASV, others
[44] Where their worm dieth not, and the fire is not quenched.	[44, 46] ———

---

54 IBID, 69–70.

55 IBID, 121.

[46] Where their worm dieth not, and the fire is not quenched.	

Mark 9:44, 46

Although it could be argued that these verses were omitted by scribes who considered the repetition to be unnecessary, such a deletion could hardly occur in manuscripts of such vast diversity as those that give witness to the absence of these verses. Contrarily, verses 44 and 46 were added as a sort of prophetic refrain that makes for good oral reading. Indeed, many textual variants entered the textual stream as the result of scribes enhancing the text for oral reading in the church. This is a classic example. Several modern English versions omit these verses and then note their inclusion for the sake of readers familiar with their place in the KJV tradition. By retaining the verses in the text, the HCSB retains the KJV tradition.[56]

Mark 11:26 King James Version (KJV)	Mark 11:26 American Standard Version (ASV), Also ESV, LEB, CSB, UASV, others
[26] But if ye do not forgive, neither will your Father which is in heaven forgive your trespasses.	[26] ———

Mark 11:26

Though it could be argued that verse 26 dropped out by a scribal mistake (both 11:25 and 11:26 end with the same three words), the WH NU reading has much better documentation than the variant. Thus, it is more likely that verse 26 is a natural scribal expansion of verse 25, borrowed from Matt 6:15, a parallel verse (cf. Matt 18:35). According to Mark's original text, Jesus was encouraging people to forgive others their trespasses against them before seeking forgiveness from God for their own trespasses. The addition makes God's forgiveness conditional. The extra verse is included in TR, followed by KJV, NKJV, as well as by NASB and HCSB, which persist in maintaining the KJV tradition. It is noted in modern versions out of deference to the KJV tradition.[57]

Mark 15:28 King James Version (KJV)	Mark 15:28 American Standard Version (ASV), Also ESV, LEB, CSB, UASV, others
[28] And the scripture was fulfilled, which saith, And he was numbered with the transgressors.	[28] ———

---

[56] IBID, 133.

[57] IBID, 142.

Mark 15:28

The documentary evidence decisively shows that this verse was not present in any Greek manuscript prior to the late sixth century (namely, 083—a manuscript discovered in the 1970s at St. Catherine's Monastery). Borrowing from a parallel passage, Luke 22:37 (which is a quotation of Isa 53:12), later scribes inserted this verse as a prophetic proof text for the phenomenon of Jesus' death with the lawless. Of all the gospel writers, Mark was by far the least concerned with showing prophetic fulfillment in the events of Jesus' life. No doubt, his Roman audience (hardly aware of the OT Scriptures) influenced this literary approach. In any event, the verse is retained in KJV and NKJV, as well as in NASB and HCSB, which usually follow KJV with respect to keeping verses in the text—in contrast to all other modern versions.[58]

Luke 17:36 King James Version (KJV)	Luke 17:36 American Standard Version (ASV), Also ESV, LEB, CSB, UASV, others
36 Two men shall be in the field; the one shall be taken, and the other left.	36 _____

Luke 17:36

Although it is possible that the verse could have been omitted due to homoeoteleuton, it is hardly possible that the mistake would have occurred in so many manuscripts of such great diversity. Therefore, it is far more likely that the verse is a scribal interpolation borrowed from Matt 24:40, with harmonization to the style of Luke 17:35. Though the verse is not present in TR, it was included in KJV (perhaps under the influence of the Latin Vulgate), NKJV, and HCSB, which in deference to KJV has a pattern of including verses that are omitted by all other modern versions.[59]

John 5:3–4 King James Version (KJV)	John 5:3–4 American Standard Version (ASV), Also ESV, LEB, CSB, UASV, others
3 In these lay a great multitude of impotent folk, of blind, halt, withered, waiting for the moving of the water.	3 In these lay a multitude of them that were sick, blind, halt, withered —— 4 _____

---

58 IBID, 154.

59 IBID, 221.

⁴ For an angel went down at a certain season into the pool, and troubled the water: whosoever then first after the troubling of the water stepped in was made whole of whatsoever disease he had.	

John 5:3b–4

This portion (5:3b–4) was probably not written by John, because it is not found in the earliest manuscripts ($\mathfrak{P}^{66}$ $\mathfrak{P}^{75}$ $\aleph$ B C* T), and where it does occur in later manuscripts it is often marked with obeli (marks like asterisks) to signal spuriousness (so Π 047 syr^h marking 5:4). The passage was a later addition—even added to manuscripts, such as A and C, that did not originally contain the portion. This scribal gloss is characteristic of the expansions that occurred in gospel texts after the fourth century. The expansion happened in two phases: First came the addition of 5:3b—inserted to explain what the sick people were waiting for; and then came 5:4—inserted to provide an explanation about the troubling of the water mentioned in 5:7. Of course, the second expansion is fuller and more imaginative. Nearly all modern textual critics and translators will not accept the longer portion as part of the original text. NASB and HCSB, however, continue to retain verses in deference to the KJV tradition.[60]

Acts 8:37 King James Version (KJV)	Acts 8:37 American Standard Version (ASV), Also ESV, LEB, CSB, UASV, others
³⁷ And Philip said, If thou believest with all thine heart, thou mayest. And he answered and said, I believe that Jesus Christ is the Son of God.	³⁷ _____

Acts 8:37

If the verse was an original part of Luke's text, there is no good reason for explaining why it would have been omitted in so many ancient manuscripts and versions. Rather, this verse is a classic example of scribal gap-filling, in that it supplied the apparent gap left by the unanswered question of the previous verse ("The eunuch said, 'Look, here is water! What is to prevent me from being baptized?' "). The interpolation puts an answer on Philip's lips that is derived from ancient Christian baptismal practices. Before being baptized, the new believer had to make a confession

---

60 IBID, 272–273.

of his or her faith in Jesus as the Son of God. A similar addition also worked its way into the text of John 9:38–39 (see note).

There is nothing doctrinally wrong with this interpolation; it affirms belief with the heart (in accordance with verses like Rom 10:9–10) and elicits the response of faith in Jesus Christ as the Son of God (in accordance with verses like John 20:31). But it is not essential that one make such a verbatim confession before being baptized. In fact, the eunuch had made no such confession, but it was obvious to Philip that he believed Jesus was the Messiah when the eunuch said, "Look, here is water. What prevents me from being baptized?" This is part of the beauty of the book of Acts: Many individuals come to faith in Christ in a variety of ways. The church throughout history has had a habit of standardizing the way people express their faith in Christ.

It is difficult to know when this interpolation first entered the text, but it could have been as early as the second century since Irenaeus (*Haer.* 3.12.8) quoted part of it. The earliest extant Greek manuscript to include it is E, of the sixth century. Erasmus included the verse in his edition of the Greek New Testament because—even though it was not present in many of the manuscripts he knew—he considered it to have been omitted by the carelessness of scribes. He based its inclusion on a marginal reading in codex 4 (see TCGNT). From Erasmus's edition, it worked its way into TR and subsequently KJV. The only reason it is printed in the margins of all the other versions is that translations invariably inform the reader about instances in which the text omits a verse that is often included in other prominent versions, especially KJV. The NASB and HCSB, with typical sensitivity to the KJV tradition, include the verse, though it is set in brackets.[61]

Acts 15:34 King James Version (KJV)	Acts 15:34 American Standard Version (ASV), Also ESV, LEB, CSB, UASV, others
[34] Notwithstanding it pleased Silas to abide there still.	[34] _____

Acts 15:34

The extra verse, though it contradicts 15:33, was added to avoid the difficulty in 15:40, which indicates that Silas was still in Antioch. Thus, in trying to solve one problem, the reviser (and other scribes) created another.

We may wonder how a verse that was not included in the Byzantine text (Maj) was incorporated into TR. The verse (in form 1) was inserted by Erasmus into his Greek text, even though he found it only in the margin of

---

[61] IBID, 363–364.

the Greek manuscripts he was using. Erasmus, probably aware of its inclusion in the Latin Vulgate, supposed that it had been omitted in the Greek manuscripts by an error of the scribes (Westcott and Hort 1882, 96). From Erasmus's text it went into TR and was then translated in KJV. Most modern versions note the omission out of deference to the KJV tradition. NASB retains the verse with a note saying that early manuscripts do not contain it.[62]

Acts 24:6–8 King James Version (KJV)	Acts 24:6–8 American Standard Version (ASV), Also ESV, LEB, CSB, UASV, others
[6] Who also hath gone about to profane the temple: whom we took, and would have judged according to our law. [7] But the chief captain Lysias came upon us, and with great violence took him away out of our hands, [8] Commanding his accusers to come unto thee: by examining of whom thyself mayest take knowledge of all these things, whereof we accuse him.	[6] who moreover assayed to profane the temple: on whom also we laid hold: —— [8] from whom thou wilt be able, by examining him thyself, to take knowledge of all these things whereof we accuse him.

Acts 24:6–8

The expanded reading, found primarily in Western manuscripts, produces a rendering of these verses in TR such as this: "[6] He even tried to profane the temple, and so we seized him. And we would have judged him according to our law. [7] But the chief captain Lysias came and with great violence took him out of our hands, [8] commanding his accusers to come before you. By examining him yourself you will be able to learn from him concerning everything of which we accuse him."

The variant reading, which found its way into the majority of manuscripts and was included in TR, is another example of gap-filling. The words are included, of course, by KJV and NKJV as well as NASB and HCSB, which often include verses that all other modern translations exclude. The words were added because a scribe did not think it likely that Felix would have received the whole story from Paul. Therefore, he connected the relative pronoun in the phrase παρ ου ("from whom") to Lysias, the tribune

---

[62] IBID, 393–394.

who rescued Paul from the Jews plotting to kill him. The same idea of using military power or force (μετα πολλης βιας) to accomplish this rescue is found in the Western addition to 23:29 (see note). But Lysias was not present to give Felix an account of these things, so the expanded variant is wrong. The text, without the interpolation, is bare but understandable: Paul was arrested so that he could now be examined and tried by Felix.[63]

Acts 28:29 King James Version (KJV)	Acts 28:29 American Standard Version (ASV), Also ESV, LEB, CSB, UASV, others
29 And when he had said these words, the Jews departed, and had great reasoning among themselves.	29 _____

Acts 28:29

The additional verse passed from the Western text into the Byzantine text. It was added to fill in the narrative gap between 28:28 and 28:30. All modern versions except NASB and HCSB do not include it in the text. Most note it out of deference to the KJV tradition.[64]

Romans 16:24 King James Version (KJV)	Romans 16:24 American Standard Version (ASV), Also ESV, LEB, CSB, UASV, others
24 The grace of our Lord Jesus Christ be with you all. Amen.	24 _____

Romans 16:24

The omission of this verse is strongly supported by all the earliest manuscripts. The verse was copied from 16:20 by some scribe (or scribes) who thought it was also suited to follow the postscript (see note on 16:20). Since TR and Majority Text include this verse, so do KJV and NKJV. The Western manuscripts (D F G) add the benediction at 16:24 because they do not include 16:25–27. All modern translations, following superior testimony, do not include the verse. At the same time, these translations provide a textual note concerning this verse because of its place in traditional English translations. The textual situation of 16:24 must be considered along with 16:25–27 (see following note).[65]

---

[63] IBID, 423–424.

[64] IBID, 433.

[65] IBID, 477.

1 John 5:7-8 King James Version (KJV, ASV) ⁷ For there are three that bear record in heaven, the Father, the Word, and the Holy Ghost: and these three are one. ⁸ And there are three that bear witness in earth, the Spirit, and the water, and the blood: and these three agree in one.	1 John 5:7-8 Updated American Standard Version (UASV), Also ESV, LEB, CSB, others ⁷ For there are three that testify: ⁸ ——

1 John 5:7b–8

John never wrote the following words: "in heaven, the Father, the Word, and the Holy Spirit: and these three are one. And there are three that bear witness in earth." This famous passage, called "the heavenly witness" or *Comma Johanneum*, came from a gloss on 5:8 which explained that the three elements (water, blood, and Spirit) symbolize the Trinity (the Father, the Word [Son], and the Spirit).

This gloss had a Latin origin (as did the one in 5:20—see note). The first time this passage appears in the longer form (with the heavenly witness) is in the treatise *Liber Apologeticus*, written by the Spanish heretic Priscillian (died ca. 385) or his follower, Bishop Instantius. Metzger said, "apparently the gloss arose when the original passage was understood to symbolize the Trinity (through the mention of the three witnesses: the Spirit, the water, and the blood), an interpretation which may have been written first as a marginal note that afterward found its way into the text" (TCGNT). The gloss showed up in the writings of Latin fathers in North Africa and Italy (as part of the text of the Epistle) from the fifth century onward, and it found its way into more and more copies of the Latin Vulgate. (The original translation of Jerome did not include it.) "The heavenly witnesses" passage has not been found in the text of any Greek manuscript prior to the fourteenth century, and it was never cited by any Greek father. Many of the Greek manuscripts listed above (in support of the variant reading) do not even include the extra verbiage in the text but rather record these words as a "variant reading" (v.r.) in the margin.

Erasmus did not include "the heavenly witnesses" passage in the first two editions of his Greek New Testament. He was criticized for this by defenders of the Latin Vulgate. Erasmus, in reply, said that he would include it if he could see it in any one Greek manuscript. In turn, a manuscript (most likely the Monfort Manuscript, 61, of the sixteenth century) was specially fabricated to contain the passage and thereby fool Erasmus. Erasmus kept his promise; he included it in the third edition. From there it became incorporated into TR and was translated in the KJV. Both KJV and NKJV have popularized this expanded passage. The NKJV translators included it in the text, knowing full well that it has no place there. This is evident in their footnote: "Only four or five very late manuscripts contain these words in Greek." Its inclusion in the text demonstrates their commitment to maintaining the KJV heritage.

Without the intrusive words, the text reads: "For there are three that testify: the Spirit, the water, and the blood; and the three are in agreement" (NIV). It has nothing to do with the Triune God, but with the three critical phases in Jesus' life where he was manifested as God incarnate, the Son of God in human form. This was made evident at his baptism (= the water), his death (= the blood), and his resurrection (= the Spirit). At his baptism, the man Jesus was declared God's beloved Son (see Matt 3:16–17). At his crucifixion, a man spilling blood was recognized by others as "God's Son" (see Mark 15:39). In the resurrection, he was designated as the Son of God in power (see Rom 1:3–4). This threefold testimony is unified in one aspect: Each event demonstrated that the man Jesus was the divine Son of God.[66]

Chapter 8 is going to give the reader even more insights into the King James Version that in all likelihood, they were not aware of but should know for salvation depends upon it.

---

[66] IBID, 784–785.

CHAPTER 19 KING JAMES VERSION
Read the Bible to Understand It

Edward D. Andrews

Above All Acquire Wisdom

Proverbs 4:7 Updated American Standard Version (UASV)

⁷ The beginning of wisdom is this: Acquire wisdom,
and with all you acquire, acquire understanding.

The beginning of wisdom is this: Acquire wisdom: Here the Hebrew has two detached phrases that are literally "the first thing of wisdom" and "get wisdom." Here King David in his advice to his son when Solomon was young was that wisdom is the most important thing, and therefore, he should pursue it so as to obtain it.

Wisdom: (Heb. *ḥāḵ·mā(h)*) is sound judgment, based on knowledge and understanding. It is the balanced application of that knowledge to answer difficulties, achieve objectives, sidestep or ward off dangers, not to mention helping others to accomplish the same. The wise person is often contrasted with the foolishness or stupid person. – Deut. 32:6; Prov. 11:29; Eccles. 6:8.

And with all you acquire, acquire understanding is again places the highest importance on obtaining or acquiring but this time it is in the pursuit of understanding or insight.

Understanding (Heb. *tᵉḇû·nā(h)*) is the ability to see how the parts or aspects of something are connected to one another. One who possesses understanding can see the big picture (the entire matter) and not just the isolated facts. – Prov. 2:5; 9:10; 18:15.

Insight (Heb. *bî·nā(h)*) is the ability to see into a situation. One who possesses insight acts with wisdom, caution, and discretion. Insight is closely related to understanding, but there is a fine distinction between the two terms. Says the *Theological Wordbook of the Old Testament:* "While *bîn* [understanding] indicates "distinguishing between," *śākal* relates to an intelligent knowledge of the reason. There is the process of thinking through a complex arrangement of thoughts resulting in a wise dealing and use of good practical common sense. Another end result is the emphasis upon being successful."[67] – Psa. 14:12.

As we learned in Proverbs chapter three, wisdom is the ability to apply knowledge and understanding effectively, to have success. Knowledge is acquired by our taking in facts that were gained by paying attention and experience, as well as through reading and study. However, all of that is useless if one cannot put that information to work for them. Insight is the ability to see into a situation. When one acts with insight, he has good sense in dealing with practical matters, using good judgment to consider likely consequences and act accordingly, as well as discretion. We are foolish if we forsake wisdom, as she will protect us from the difficulties of this system of things, but that protection only comes to those that remain loyal in our love for her. If we lack wisdom, then we must begin to pursue it, in addition to insight.

The education of an Israelite child was taken very seriously, as Jehovah himself commanded that parent, "You shall teach them [the law] diligently to your sons and shall talk of them when you sit in your house and when you walk by the way and when you lie down and when you rise up." (Deut. 6:7) However, before they were to teach their child, it was commanded: "these words, which I am commanding you today, shall be on your heart." (Deut. 6:6) As Deuteronomy, 6:7 made quite clear there is no excuse for not spending time with your child and passing on wisdom and insight is paramount.

Acquire wisdom, and with all you acquire, acquire understanding. commands King David to his young son Solomon. How can you apply this counsel to our Bible reading? The Bible of sixty-six books is the only book to be authored by God as he used 40+ men, moving them along with the Holy Spirit as they wrote. The Bible contains God's thoughts. There is more to acquiring God's thoughts than merely reading the printed words on a page. We must understand what we read. Moreover, we must understand what the author meant by the words that were used, as opposed to interjecting what we feel, think, or believe God meant by those words. So, we need to meditatively read, study, and research the Bible, then, acquiring an understanding of what God meant to convey to us by the words of wisdom that he used.

One way that we can know whether we are reading, studying, and researching the Bible to understand the words of wisdom correctly is to ask

---

[67] R. Laird Harris, Gleason L. Archer Jr., and Bruce K. Waltke, eds., *Theological Wordbook of the Old Testament* (Chicago: Moody Press, 1999), 877.

ourselves what translation of the Bible are we using and why are we using this particular Bible? Are we using it because it is an easy to understand translation (CEV, GNT, NLT, NIV, etc.)? Or, are we using it because it is familiar to us and we are accustomed to using it (KJV)? Or are we using it because we know it is accurate and faithful to the original text and it is going to give us what God said by way of his human authors, not what a translator thinks God meant in its place? (ASV, RSV, NASB, CSB, NASB, and especially the UASV)[68] In chapters 5-7, we already discussed using the dynamic equivalent, interpretive, easy to understand translations.

In chapter 8, we had earnestly begun the discussion of using the King James Version. Here we continue with the most widely used English translation of the Bible, the King James Version, which most readers use because are familiar with it and unfamiliar with modern translations, mainly because they refuse to give modern translations a hearing ear. Some prefer the beautiful Shakespearean language, possibly, and do not want to see it changed. In many cases, they are unknowingly reading the Bible more for its literary effect than for understanding. Or, they have mistakenly thought that the King James Version is itself inspired by God, unchanged, error-free, and authorized. In the previous chapter, Do You Really Know the King James Version, we learned that there is no sound basis for any Christian to believe that the King James Version is itself inspired by God, unchanged, error-free, and authorized.

Considering that the Bible was written originally in written Hebrew, Aramaic, and Greek; then, translation into today's modern languages is necessary. Thus, we have seen in the past few decades many modern translations of the Bible, with there now being over 100 English translations alone. Here again, the most used English Bible being the King James Version was published over four hundred years ago in 1611, which makes it the most dated (out of date, archaic) translation that we have. In 1611, the language was modern and up to date. However, language changes in decades, let alone centuries. As a result, the readers of the King James Version believe that they know and understand what they are reading but they are really failing to understand it fully. This is very serious. These devoted Christians have exhibited a willful blindness to the truth about translation.

Language Changes Obscure Understanding

As we have noted hundreds of years have passed since the days of King James hundreds of English words have changed in meaning or have

_____

[68] https://www.uasvbible.org/

taken on new meanings, even the opposite of what was meant in 1611. When these modern-day readers of the King James Version come across these words, they obscure their understanding of what the author meant, while the reader of four hundred years ago readily understood them the right way. How sad that these changes in the meaning of words have unknowingly caused confusion and blocked understanding to a people so dedicated to the Word of God.

Conversation

1 Peter 3:1-2 King James Version (KJV)	1 Peter 3:1-2 English Standard Version (ESV)	1 Peter 3:1-2 New American Standard Bible (NASB)	1 Peter 3:1-2 Updated American Standard Version (UASV)
3 Likewise, ye wives, be in subjection to your own husbands; that, if any obey not the word, they also may without the word be won by the **conversation** of the wives; ² While they behold your **chaste <u>conversation</u>** coupled with fear.	3 Likewise, wives, be subject to your own husbands, so that even if some do not obey the word, they may be won without a word by the **conduct** of their wives, ² when they see your **respectful and pure <u>conduct</u>**.	3 In the same way, you wives, be submissive to your own husbands so that even if any *of them* are disobedient to the word, they may be won without a word by the **behavior** of their wives, ² as they observe your **chaste and respectful <u>behavior</u>**.	3 In the same way, you wives, be submissive to your own husbands so that even if any of them are disobedient to the word, they may be won without a word by the **behavior** of their wives, ² as they observe your **chaste and respectful <u>behavior</u>**.

Today, the word **conversation** is the informal exchange of ideas by spoken words. Consequently, how are modern readers of the King James Version to understand the apostle Paul's counsel to Christian wives that unbelieving husbands may be won over to the faith "**by the <u>conversation</u> of the wives**; While they behold your **chaste conversation** coupled with fear." Now, what does that even mean, really? Does it mean that Christian wives can win over their unbelieving husbands through conversation, the exchange of ideas? And must a Christian wife **fear** her husband?

Now, the King James Version reader believe that they know what the word **conversation** and the word **fear** mean so they come away with the wrong understanding of what Paul meant by the Greek words that he used. Why can we say this with certainty? Because the word conversation meant something completely different four hundred years ago. In 1611, the word conversation meant, "General course of manners; behavior; deportment; especially as it respects morals."[69] Now that we have a better understanding of the koine (common) Greek of the first century, we know the Greek noun (*anastrophē*) means "**behavior**, way of life, one's conduct in life (Gal 1:13; Eph 4:22; Heb 13:7; 1Pe 1:15; 3:1; 2Pe 3:11)"[70] Yes, the meaning is of a person's moral conduct or behavior, which means that an unbelieving husband can "be won without a word by the **behavior** of their wives."

In addition, the husband is not won over by the **fear** of the wife but rather as the Greek noun (*phobos*) says, profound respect or chaste respect. Yes, it is true that the primary meaning of *phobos* is **fear**. However, as we all know today, Greek is like all other languages and ever word has several different meanings. "**phobos**; from φέβομαι phebomai *(to be put to flight); panic flight, fear, the causing of fear, terror.* – cause of fear (1), fear (37), fearful (1), fears (1), intimidation (1), respect (1), respectful (1), reverence (1), sense of awe (1)."[71] A modern-day English example would be the word hand, it has 24 different meanings, such as the end part of a person's arm beyond the wrist, but also the hand on a clock, a hand of cards, the hand (worker) on an oil rig, and many more. The meaning is according to the context. If the context was the **hand** of God, the meaning would be the power of God, another one of the twenty-four different meanings.

---

[69] KJV Dictionary (Thursday, August 9, 2018) https://av1611.com/kjbp/kjv-dictionary/

[70] James Swanson, *Dictionary of Biblical Languages with Semantic Domains: Greek (New Testament)* (Oak Harbor: Logos Research Systems, Inc., 1997).

[71] Robert L. Thomas, *New American Standard Hebrew-Aramaic and Greek Dictionaries: Updated Edition* (Anaheim: Foundation Publications, Inc., 1998).

1 Corinthians 10:24-25 King James Version (KJV)	1 Corinthians 10:24-25 English Standard Version (ESV)	1 Corinthians 10:24-25 New American Standard Bible (NASB)	1 Corinthians 10:24-25 Updated American Standard Version (UASV)
[24] Let no man **seek** his own, but **every man another's wealth.** [25] Whatsoever is sold in the **shambles**, that eat, asking no question for conscience sake:	[24] Let no one seek his own good, but **the good of his neighbor.** [25] Eat whatever is sold in the **meat market** without raising any question on the ground of conscience.	[24] Let no one **seek** his own *good*, but that **of his neighbor.** [25] Eat anything that is sold in the **meat market** without asking questions for conscience' sake;	[24] Let each one **keep seeking,** not his own **good,** but that **of the other person.** [25] Eat whatever is sold in the **meat market** without raising questions for the sake of conscience.

The King James Version reader is likely wondering what did Paul mean by **seeking another man's wealth**? Moreover, what is **shambles**? What kind of food might one buy at a shambles? In 1611, shambles meant "The place where butcher's meat is sold; a meat market." Yes, the Greek noun (*makellon*) means "**meat market**, food market (1Co 10:25+)."[72] How much clearer the understanding is now. Of course, the King James Version preacher has likely been giving the modern-day reader the meaning of shambles by saying, *shambles or meat market*, as he gives his sermon. Yet, this does not take away that there are over one thousand words in the King James Version that do not mean today what they meant in 1611. For goodness sake, they have a King James Version dictionary. (av1611.com) Lastly, on this verse, we do not seek another man's wealth but rather we keep seeking the good of the other person.

---

[72] James Swanson, *Dictionary of Biblical Languages with Semantic Domains: Greek (New Testament)* (Oak Harbor: Logos Research Systems, Inc., 1997).

Addicted

1 Corinthians 16:15 King James Version (KJV)	1 Corinthians 16:15 English Standard Version (ESV)	1 Corinthians 16:15 New American Standard Bible (NASB)	1 Corinthians 16:15 Updated American Standard Version (UASV)
[15] I beseech you, brethren, (ye know the house of Stephanas, that it is the firstfruits of Achaia, and that they have **addicted** themselves to the ministry of the saints,)	[15] Now I urge you, brothers— you know that the household of Stephanas were the first converts in Achaia, and that they have **devoted** themselves to the service of the saints	[15] Now I urge you, brethren (you know the household of Stephanas, that they were the first fruits of Achaia, and that they have **devoted** themselves for ministry to the saints),	[15] Now I urge you, brothers, you know that the household of Stephanas were the first converts in Achaia, and that they have **devoted** themselves to ministering to the holy ones,

Addicted today means *to be physically and mentally dependent* on a particular substance, and unable to stop taking it without incurring adverse effects. However, four hundred years ago, addicted meant *devoted by customary practice*. The Greek verb (*tassō*) means "**give oneself to**, do with devotion (1Co 16:15+)."[73] Yes, the household of Stephanas "**devoted** themselves to ministering to the holy ones," as opposed to the modern understanding of '**addicting** themselves to the ministry of the saints.' Below we have borrowed some entries from the King James Version Bible to move along faster, briefer, so you can see the impact in greater detail. Remember, this is but a handful of words out of more than a thousand.

Sottish Children

Sottish, a word used at Jeremiah 4:22, meaning foolish or stupid children.

---

[73] James Swanson, *Dictionary of Biblical Languages with Semantic Domains: Greek (New Testament)* (Oak Harbor: Logos Research Systems, Inc., 1997).

Overcharge

Overcharge, a word used at 2 Corinthians 2:5, meaning not to say too much, not to exaggerate, not to put it too severely, not to be too harsh.

shall not prevent them

Shall not prevent them, at 1 Thessalonians 4:15 means will not precede those

Space does not allow further discussion of how language in the *King James Version* blocks understanding, but here is a list of a few more examples, together with the word or phrase used by modern translations to enable us to get the meaning that God wanted us to get.

KING JAMES VERSION	ASV, RSV, NRSV, ESV, CSB, UASV, others	BIBLE TEXT
alleging	proving	Acts 17:3
anon	Immediately, at once	Mark 1:30
barbarous	Natives, local people, foreign-speaking people	Acts 28:2
charger	platter	Matthew 14:11
charity	love	1 Corinthians 13:13
cheek teeth	fangs	Joel 1:6
confectionaries	perfume makers, perfumers	1 Samuel 8:13
divers places	various places	Matthew 24:7
drunken	is drunk	1 Corinthians 11:21
leasing	lies	Psalm 4:2
mortify	put to death	Romans 8:13
outlandish women	foreign women	Nehemiah 13:26
publican	tax collector	Matthew 10:3
sons of Belial	Worthless, (lit. *sons of Belial*)	1 Samuel 2:12
sod pottage	was cooking, cooked	Genesis 25:29
suffer	let, permit	Mark 10:14

take no thought	do not be anxious	Matthew 10:19
turtle	turtledove	Song of Solomon 2:12
unicorn	wild ox	Numbers 23:22
winked at	overlooked	Acts 17:30
do you to wit	make known	2 Corinthians 8:1
wotteth not	does not know	Genesis 39:8

Correctly understanding God's Word is the thing of the highest importance. Using the King James Version for a long time, being familiar with the King James Version, family tradition, sentimentality, should not overshadow the importance of understanding what the author meant by the words that were used. As God instructed King David, who counseled young Solomon and by extension us, **with all you acquire, acquire understanding**, which places the highest importance on obtaining or acquiring in our pursuit of understanding or having insight into God's Word.

Many of you readers have been using only the *King James Version* of the Bible. The wise course here is to **acquire** a translation that will bring the meaning of God's Word to you in the most understandable form. We recommend that you Investigate the English Standard Version (ESV), the Lexham English Bible (LEB), the Christian Standard Bible (CSB), the New American Standard Bible (NASB) while you await the full release of the Updated American Standard Version (UASV) – www.uasvbible.org/.

Chapter 9 will not get into the development of the master texts (critical texts) that developed after the Textus Receptus.

CHAPTER 20 The Reign of the King James Version Is Over

Edward D. Andrews

Exactly why are we making other translations beyond the King James Version of 1611? The King James Version has been the primary translation of the Christian community for 400 years (1611-2011). There is no doubt that this Bible alone has affected the lives of hundreds of millions and has influenced the principles of Bible translation for the past four centuries.

Before we delve into what makes for a good translation, let us pause to consider the translation policy of the KJV translation committee. We can hardly talk about the KJV without looking at the translator William Tyndale (1494-1536), the man who published the first printed New Testament from the original language of Greek. In the face of much persecution, William Tyndale of England followed with his English translation of Erasmus' Greek New Testament text, completing this while in exile on the continent of Europe in 1525.

Tyndale respected and treasured the Bible. However, in his days, the religious leaders insisted on keeping it in Latin, a language that had been dead for centuries. Therefore, with the purpose of making it available to his fellow citizens, Tyndale was determined to translate the Bible into English. While the idea of Bible translation being against the law may be unfamiliar to the modern mind, this was not the case in Tyndale's day. He was educated at Oxford University and became an esteemed instructor at The Cambridge University. Because of his desire to bring the common man the Bible in English, he had to flee from his academic career, escaping the Continent. His life became one of a fugitives, but he managed to complete the New Testament and some of the Old Testament, before he was finally arrested, imprisoned for heresy, and strangled at the stake, with his body being burned afterward.

Tyndale's work sparked a widespread translation project that produced a new revision every couple of years, or so it seemed. The Coverdale Bible of 1536, the Matthew's Bible of 1537, the Great Bible of 1539, the Taverner's Bible of 1539, the Geneva Bible of 1560 (went through 140 editions), the Edmund Becke's Bible of 1549, the Bishop's Bible of 1568, and the Rheims-Douay Bible of 1610. The King James Version is a revision of all these translations, as they too were of their predecessor, the Tyndale translation. The KJV translation committee was ordered to use the Bishop's Bible as their foundation text and was not to alter it unless Tyndale, Coverdale, Matthew, Cranmer or the Great Bible, and the Geneva agreed, and then they were to assume that reading. Thus, the King James Version is unquestionably 90 percent William Tyndale's translation.

There is no other translation, which possesses more literary beauty than the King James Version. However, there are several reasons as to why there was a need to revise the King James Version. The **first reason** is the **King James Version's** textual basis, which is from the period of 1611. The Greek text behind the KJV New Testament is what is known as the Textus Receptus, a corrupt Greek text produced by a scholar in the 16th-century, Desiderius Erasmus. Concerning this text, Dr. Bruce Metzger wrote that it was "a handful of late and haphazardly collected minuscule manuscripts and in a dozen passages its reading is supported by no Greek witnesses." (Metzger 2003, 106) While most of the corruptions are considered insignificant, others are significant, such as 1 Timothy 3:16; 1 John 5:7; John 7:53-8:11; and Mark 16:9-20. However, we cannot lay the blame at the feet of the translation committee of the KJV, for they did not have the textual evidence that we possess today.

The **second reason** is that the **KJV** comes from the 17th-century and contains many archaic words that either obscure the meaning or mislead its reader: "howbeit," "thee," "thy," "thou," "thine," and "shambles." An example of misleading can be found in the word "let," which meant to "stop," "hinder" or "restrain" in 1611, but today means "to allow" or "to permit." Therefore, when the KJV says that Paul 'let the great apostasy come into the church,' it is completely misleading to the modern mind. In 1611 "let" meant that he 'restrained or prevented the apostasy.' (2 Thess. 2:7) The KJV at Mark 6:20 inform us "Herod feared John, knowing that he was a just man and an holy, and observed him." Actually, the Greek behind "observed him" means that Herod "kept him safe."

The **third reason** is that the **KJV** contains translation errors. However, like the first reason, it is not the fault of the translators, as Hebrew and Greek were just resurfacing as subjects of serious study after the Dark Ages. The discovery of papyrus writings in Egypt, in the late 19th and early 20th centuries, has helped us better to understand the common (Koine) Greek of the first century C.E. These discoveries have shown that everyday words were not understood as well as had been thought. The KJV at Matthew 5:22 informs the reader "whosoever is angry with his brother without a cause shall be in danger of the judgment: and whosoever shall say to his brother, Raca, shall be in danger of the council ..." The ESV renders it, "whoever insults his brother will be liable (a term of abuse) to the council ..." Scholar Walter C. Kaiser has said, "the actual insult mentioned by Jesus is the word 'Raca' as it stands in the KJV. The precise meaning of 'Raca' is disputed; it is probably an Aramaic word meaning something like 'imbecile' but was plainly regarded as a deadly insult."

The **fourth reason** is that the **KJV** has over a thousand words in it that do not mean today what they meant in 1611. Words change over time, some even meaning the opposite. For example, the word "let," as used in the King James Version, meant 'to stop,' 'to prevent,' or 'to restrain' in 1611. Today "let" means 'to allow,' 'to permit,' or 'consent to. Thus, in 1611, when the KJV was published, 2 Thessalonians said that Paul "let" the great apostasy come into the church, which meant that Paul actually "stopped" or "restrained" the great apostasy from coming into the church. Now, those who do not know that in 1611 "let" meant, "prevent," "stop," and "restrain" in 1611, it was correctly translated. However, today, the English reader would be getting the opposite meaning from that 2 Thessalonians 2:7.

2 Thessalonians 2:7 Updated American Standard Version (UASV)	2 Thessalonians 2:7 King James Version (KJV)
[7] For the mystery[74] of lawlessness is already at work; but only until the one who is right now acting as a restraint is out of the way.	[7] For the mystery of iniquity doth already work: only he who now letteth will let, until he be taken out of the way.

The translators that have come after the King James Version can draw much direction in what makes a worthy translation by considering the principles of translation that were followed in the production of the world's most influential Bible. The translators endeavored to discover the corresponding English word for the actual original language word of Hebrew and Greek.

According to Alister McGrath, the translators felt obligated to . . .

- Ensure that every word in the original was rendered by an English equivalent;

- Make it clear when they added any words to make the sense clearer, or to lead to better English . . .

- Follow the basic word order of the original wherever possible.[75]

---

[74] **Mystery; Secret:** (Gr. *mystērion*) A sacred divine mystery or secret doctrine that lies with God alone, which is withheld from both the angelic body and humans, until the time he determines that it is to be revealed, and to those to whom he chooses to make it known.– Mark 4:11; Rom. 11:25; 16:25; 1 Cor. 2:1; 4:1; 13:2; 14:2; 15:51; Eph. 1:9; 6:19; Col. 1:26; 2:2; 2 Thess. 2:7; 1 Tim. 3:9; Rev. 17:5.

[75] McGrath, Alister. *In the Beginning: The Story of the King James Bible and How It Changed a Nation, a Language, and a Culture.* New York: Anchor, 2002, p. 250.

There is any number of ways that each one of us may have been drawn into the field of Bible translation differences, the translation process, and textual criticism. It might be that some have been using the King James Version their entire life and with all of these new translations reading differently, especially in the New Testament, they began investigating why. Maybe it is the opposite, and we are using a more recent English translation such as the NASB, ESV, HCSB, LEB or the UASV. Then, maybe we have had a number of persons, who are commonly called the King James Version Only tell us that the KJV is based on the best and oldest Greek manuscripts, saying our translation is corrupt. Thus, in either of the above scenarios, we began by comparing the King James Version with some of the New Translations. We began to discover many differences between the new translations and the King James Version, which made us wonder, which is correct? We wonder, "Is the Bible that I have been using even accurate?" or "How can I know which Bible translation is most accurate?" Below are but a few examples **out of hundreds** of what would be discovered upon such an investigation. In our examples, we have chosen to compare the King James Version (KJV, 1611) against the Updated American Standard Version (UASV, 2016). Keep in mind that the 1901 ASV, the 1952 RSV, the 1995 NASB, and the 2001 ESV are going to read similar to the UASV because they too are literal translations based on the latest and best evidence. (some not as literal as the UASV, e.g., the ESV, RSV) The **Textus Receptus** (i.e., received text) is the name given to the printed Greek text of the New Testament, which served as the basis for the original German Luther Bible (1522), the translation of the New Testament into English by William Tyndale (1526), the King James Version (1611), and most other New Testament translations of the Reformation era. The critical Greek texts of the New Testament, which has served as the basis for modern-day translations, including the ESV, are the Westcott and Hort Text of 1881, the United Bible Society (UBS5, 2014), and the Nestle-Aland (NA28, 2012).[76] Material within brackets [   ] means the reading was not in the original text.

Matthew 5:44

KJV: But I say unto you, Love your enemies, bless them that curse you, do good to them that hate you, and pray for them which despitefully use you, and persecute you;

UASV: But I say to you, Love your enemies and pray for those who persecute you,

---

[76] The primary difference between the UBS5 and the NA28 is that translators primarily use the latter, while textual scholars primarily use the former.

[do good to them that hate you, and pray for them which despitefully use you, and persecute you;] The shorter reading in the ESV is found in the more trusted manuscripts from the fourth century while the longer reading of the KJV is found in manuscripts of the fifth century and beyond. The shorter reading is found in the citation of earlier church fathers while later church fathers cited the longer reading. It seems a copyist borrowed the above words from Luke 6:27-28, adding them to Matthew.

Matthew 6:13

KJV: And lead us not into temptation, but deliver us from evil: For thine is the kingdom, and the power, and the glory, forever. Amen.

UASV: And lead us not into temptation, but deliver us from evil.

[For thine is the kingdom, and the power, and the glory, forever. Amen.] The manuscript evidence is against the longer reading being original. It likely came from the *Didache* (aka, The Teaching of the Twelve Apostles) which is a brief early Christian source on traditions of the church, dated by most scholars to the early second century.

Matthew 17:21

KJV: Howbeit this kind goeth not out but by prayer and fasting.

UASV: The verse was omitted because of the substantial manuscript evidence led to the conclusion that this verse was not in the original text.

Bruce M. Metzger observes, "There is no satisfactory reason why the passage, if originally present in Matthew, should have been omitted in a wide variety of witnesses, and ... copyists frequently inserted material derived from another Gospel ..."[77]

Matthew 18:11

KJV: For the Son of man is come to save that which was lost.

UASV: The verse was omitted because it was absent from several important and diverse manuscripts, evidencing that this verse was not in the original text.

On this verse, Metzger writes, "There can be little doubt that the words [from the longer reading] are spurious here, being absent from the earliest witnesses representing several textual types (Alexandrian, Egyptian, Antiochian), and manifestly borrowed by copyists from Lk 19:10. The

---

[77] Bruce Manning Metzger, United Bible Societies, *A Textual Commentary on the Greek New Testament, Second Edition a Companion Volume to the United Bible Societies' Greek New Testament (4th Rev. Ed.)* (London; New York: United Bible Societies, 1994), 35.

reason for the interpolation was apparently to provide a connection between ver. 10 and verses 12–14."[78]

What Was a Pim?

1 Samuel 13:21 King James Version (KJV)

[21] Yet they had a file [Heb., *pim*] for the mattocks, and for the coulters, and for the forks, and for the axes, and to sharpen the goads.

1 Samuel 13:21 Updated American Standard Version (UASV)

[21] The charge was a pim for the plowshares and for the mattocks, for the three-pronged fork, for the axes, and for fixing the oxgoad.

1 Samuel 13:21 English Standard Version (ESV)

[21] and the charge was two-thirds of a shekel for the plowshares and for the mattocks, and a third of a shekel for sharpening the axes and for setting the goads.

1 Samuel 13:21 New American Standard Bible (NASB)

[21] The charge was two-thirds of a shekel for the plowshares, the mattocks, the forks, and the axes, and to fix the hoes.

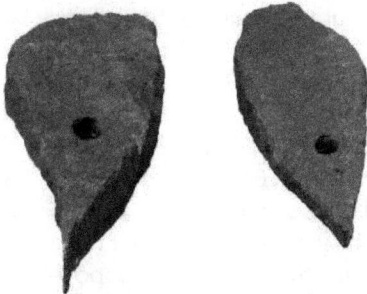

What was a pim? It would not be uncovered until 1907 when archaeology discovered the first pim weight stone at the ancient city of Gezer. The translation, like the above King James Version, struggled in their translation of the word "pim." Today, translators know that the pim was a weight measure of about 7.82 grams, or as the English Standard Version has it, "two-thirds of a shekel," a common Hebrew unit of weight that the Philistines charged for sharpening the Israelites plowshares and mattocks.

What is the Mystery of Godliness?

1 Timothy 3:16 Updated American Standard Version (UASV)	1 Timothy 3:16 King James Version (KJV)
[16] And confessedly, great is the mystery of godliness:	[16] And without controversy great is the mystery of godliness: **God was**

---

[78] IBID, 36

He was manifested in the flesh, vindicated in the Spirit, seen by angels, proclaimed among the nations, believed on in the world, taken up in glory.	manifest in the flesh, justified in the Spirit, seen of angels, preached unto the Gentiles, believed on in the world, received up into glory.

The word translated God was originally abbreviated ΘC (the nomen sacrum for θεός), which had originally looked like the Greek word OC (i.e., ὅς), the latter meaning "who." Metzger makes the following observation, "The reading θεός arose either (a) accidentally, through the misreading of OC as ΘC, or (b) deliberately, either to supply a substantive for the following six verbs or, with less probability, to provide greater dogmatic precision." (p. 574) Point (a) that it was an accidental misreading of OC as ΘC and that it was unlikely to be intentional, for doctrinal purposes, seems a bit dismissive. Nevertheless, this has long been the position of many scholars.

In fact, Johann Jakob Wettstein (1693-1754) noticed that ΘC, had originally looked like OC, but felt that a horizontal stroke had faintly shown through the other side of the uncial manuscript page, contributing to a later hand adding a horizontal line to OC, giving us the contraction ΘC ("God"). However, this author believes that Philip W. Comfort makes a valid point, when he writes, "It is difficult to imagine how several fourth-and-fifth-century scribes, who had seen thousands of nomina sacra, would have made this mistake. It is more likely that the changes were motivated by a desire to make the text say that it was "God" who was manifested in the flesh." (P. W. Comfort 2008, 663) If we believe that doctrinal considerations were not behind the scribal changes, all we have to do is investigate what took place when it was understood that the actual reading was "He who was manifested in the flesh," as opposed to "God was manifested in the flesh." The battle in the nineteenth century was as though the loss of the reading in the Textus Receptus (θεός KJV) would undermine the doctrine of the Trinity. Doctrinal motivations have always played a role in the copying of the Bible, but the truth is these are actually few in number. Considering the number of manuscripts that were copied, if this were a major problem, we should see more.

Scribal Interpolations

1 John 5:7-8 (WHNU)	1 John 5:7-8 (TR)
7 οτι τρεις εισιν οι μαρτυρουντες 8 το πνευμα και το υδωρ και το αιμα και οι τρεις εις το εν εισιν	7 οτι τρεις εισιν οι μαρτυρουντες **εν τω ουρανω ο πατηρ ο λογος και το αγιον πνευμα και ουτοι οι τρεις εν εισιν** 8 **και τρεις εισιν οι μαρτυρουντες εν τη γη** το πνευμα και το υδωρ και το αιμα και οι τρεις εις το εν εισιν
1 John 5:7-8 (UASV)	**1 John 5:7-8 (KJV)**
7 For there are three that testify:[79] 8 the Spirit and the water and the blood; and the three are in agreement.	7 For there are three that bear record **in heaven, the Father, the Word, and the Holy Ghost: and these three are one.** 8 And there are three that bear witness **in earth**, the Spirit, and the water, and the blood: and these three agree in one.

In verse 7 of 1 John 5, after μαρτυροῦντες (testify), the Textus Receptus adds, ἐν τῷ οὐρανῷ, ὁ Πατήρ, ὁ Λόγος, καὶ τὸ Ἅγιον Πνεῦμα· καὶ οὗτοι οἱ τρεῖς ἕν εἰσι (in heaven, the Father, the Word, and the Holy Ghost: and these three are one). In verse 8, the Textus Receptus has καὶ τρεῖς εἰσιν οἱ μαρτυροῦντες ἐν τῇ γῇ (And there are three that bear witness in earth). There is no doubt that these words are an interpolation into the text, which textual scholarship has long known.

These additional words are missing from every Greek manuscript except eight, the earliest being from the tenth century. Metzger offers that these eight

After μαρτυροῦντες, the Textus Receptus adds the following: ἐν τῷ οὐρανῷ, ὁ Πατήρ, ὁ Λόγος, καὶ τὸ Ἅγιον Πνεῦμα· καὶ οὗτοι οἱ τρεῖς ἕν εἰσι. (8) καὶ τρεῖς εἰσιν οἱ μαρτυροῦντες ἐν τῇ γῇ. That these words are spurious

---

[79] A few late MSS add ... in heaven, the Father, the Word, and the Holy Spirit, and these three are one. (8) And there are three that testify on earth, the Spirit

and have no right to stand in the New Testament is certain in the light of the following considerations. "Contain the passage in what appears to be a translation from a late recension of the Latin Vulgate. Four of the eight manuscripts contain the passage as a variant reading written in the margin as a later addition to the manuscript." (TCGNT, 649)

In addition, the added words were not quoted by any of the Greek Fathers. Certainly, had they been aware of these words, there is little doubt that they would have referenced them repeatedly in the fourth century Trinitarian debates. Metzger tells us that "Its first appearance in Greek is in a Greek version of the (Latin) Acts of the Lateran Council in 1215." (TCGNT, 649)

The interpolation is also missing from all the manuscripts of the ancient versions, with the exception of the Latin (Syriac, Coptic, Armenian, Ethiopic, Arabic, and Slavonic). However, it is not found in the Old Latin in its earliest form (Tertullian Cyprian Augustine). Moreover, it is not present in "the Vulgate (*b*) as issued by Jerome (codex Fuldensis [copied a.d.541–46] and codex Amiatinus [copied before a.d. 716]) or (*c*) as revised by Alcuin (first hand of codex Vallicellianus [ninth century])." (TCGNT, 649)

This interpolation had its beginning in Latin, in the treatise Liber Apologetics, which was written by the Spanish heretic Priscillian (d. c. 385), bishop of Ávila, or his follower, Bishop Instantius. Metzger writes, "Apparently the gloss arose when the original passage was understood to symbolize the Trinity (through the mention of three witnesses: the Spirit, the water, and the blood), an interpretation that may have been written first as a marginal note that afterward found its way into the text. In the fifth century the gloss was quoted by Latin Fathers in North Africa and Italy as part of the text of the Epistle, and from the sixth century onwards it is found more and more frequently in manuscripts of the Old Latin and of the Vulgate." (TCGNT, 649)

Think about it, if these interpolations were original, there would be no reason to remove them, and they would be found in our earliest and best manuscripts, as well as hundreds of years of copying. Moreover, there would be no reason for their being missing from the versions either. Lastly, the interpolation also interrupts the sense.

Both a Science and an Art

We said at the outset that New Testament textual criticism is both a science and an art. Throughout almost all of this publication, we have used the science aspect, in that we have spoken of and applied many of the rules and principles. However, we will offer one verse here where the art aspect comes into play; we must not be rigid in our application of the rules and principles, meaning that we must be balanced.

Mark 1:41 (TR WHNU)	Mark 1:41 (LEB NEB REB)
σπλαγχνισθεις εκτεινας την χειρα αυτου ηψατο	οργισθεις εκτεινας την χειρα αυτου ηψατο
(‭א‬ A B C L W f¹,¹³ 33 565 700 syr cop Diatessaron)	(D a, d, ff²)

Mark 1:41 (NASB)	Mark 1:41 (LEB)
⁴¹ Moved with compassion [*splanchnon*], Jesus stretched out His hand and touched him	⁴¹ And becoming angry [*orgistheis*], he stretched out his hand *and* touched *him*

The reason that this text is considered difficult is because of one having to go against the grain of the textual principles: *Which reading is it that the other reading(s) most likely came from?* Well, it is certainly easy to see how "moved with anger" would have been changed to "move with pity." In that case, the scribe would have been softening the reading. It is very difficult to understand why a scribe would be tempted to go from "move with pity" to "moved with anger." On the other hand, the textual evidence for "moved with pity" is very weighty, while the textual evidence "moved with anger" has no real weight at all. Most persons who define textual criticism say, 'it is an art and a science.' What they mean is that it is a science in that there are rules and principles, like the ones above, and it is an art, because one needs to be balanced in the application of those rules and principles. The textual rule of which reading is it that the others came from is not to be rigidly applied; there are times that it does not apply, this being one of them.

First, the Western text **D**, which gives us the reading of "moved with anger," is notorious for making "significant" changes to the text. Comfort and Metzger, as well as others, offer a very real reason as to why the scribe may have chosen to do so. "He may have decided to make Jesus angry with the leper for wanting a miracle—in keeping with the tone of voice Jesus used in 1:43 when he sternly warned the leper." (P. W. Comfort 2008, 98) However, as Comfort goes on to point out, this would have been a misunderstanding on the part of the scribe, because Jesus was not warning him about seeking a miracle, it was rather "a warning about keeping the miracle a secret." Another motive for the scribe to alter the text to the harder reading is because he felt the man was slow to believe that Jesus was serious about healing him (v. 40) In addition, why would the scribes soften the text here from "move with anger" to "moved with pity," but not do the same at Mark 3:12 and 10:14? Let us revisit Erasmus and build on his account, moving on to the critical text.

We can grow in knowledge and understanding of how the Greek New Testament came down to us. If we cannot defend the Bible how can we defend the faith? It is not about winning arguments; it is about winning misguided souls that have been misinformed (1 Pet 3:15) and saving those who have begun to doubt. (Jude 1:22-23)

Why We Can Have Confidence?

The art and science of textual criticism and related areas like paleography go back hundreds of years. Over the last 140-years, textual research has become more certain and exact every year. And each new literal Bible translation that builds upon this foundation in an honest impartial manner, becomes purer and more accurate. Thus, the last 400 years, especially the last 140-years can give us complete confidence that the literal Bible translations are a mirror-like reflection of the originals, the unaltered Word of God.

Chapter 11 will go into an idea that most have never pondered. Do we need to find the original manuscripts to have the originals?

CHAPTER 21 The Revised Version (1881-1895)

Frederic G. Kenyon

The TEXT OF THE NEW TESTAMENT describes the process of accumulation of materials which began with the coming of the Codex Alexandrinus to London in 1625 and continues to the present day, and the critical use made of these materials in the 19th century; and the story need not be repeated here. It was not until the progress of criticism had revealed the defective state of the received Greek text of the New Testament that any movement arose for the revision of the Authorized Version. About the year 1855 the question began to be mooted in magazine articles and motions in Convocation and by way of bringing it to a head a small group of scholars (Dr. Ellicott, afterwards bishop of Gloucester, Dr. Moberly, headmaster of Winchester and afterwards bishop of Salisbury, Dr. Barron, principal of St. Edmund's Hall, Oxford, the Rev. H. Alford, afterwards Dean of Canterbury, and the Rev. W.G. Humphrey; with the Rev. E. Hawkins, secretary of the S.P.G., and afterwards canon of Westminster, as their secretary) undertook a revision of the Authorized Version of John, which was published in 1857. Six of the Epistles followed in 1861 and 1863, by which time the object of the work, in calling attention to the need and the possibility of a revision, had been accomplished. Meanwhile, a great stimulus to the interest in textual criticism had been given by the discovery of the Codex Sinaiticus, and by the work of Tischendorf and Tregelles. In February 1870 a motion for a committee to consider the desirableness of a revision was adopted by both houses of the Convocation of Canterbury, and definite motions in favor of such a revision were passed in the following May. The Convocation of York did not concur, and thenceforth the Southern Houses proceeded alone. A committee of both houses drew up the lists of revisers and framed the rules for their guidance. The Old Testament company consisted of 25 (afterwards 27) members, the New Testament of 26. The rules prescribed the introduction of as few alterations in the Authorized Version as possible consistently with faithfulness; the text to be adopted for which the evidence is decidedly preponderating, and when it differs from that from which the Authorized Version was made, the alteration to be indicated in the margin (this rule was found impracticable); alterations to be made on the first revision by simple majorities, but to be retained only if passed by a two-thirds majority on the second revision. Both companies commenced work at Westminster on June 22, 1870. The New Testament company met on 407 days in the course of eleven years, the Old Testament company on 792 days in fifteen years. Early in the work, the cooperation of American scholars was invited, and in consequence two companies of 15 and 16 members respectively were formed, which began work in 1872, considering the results of the English revision as each section of it was forwarded to them. The collaboration of the English and American companies was perfectly harmonious; and by agreement, those recommendations of the American Revisers which were not adopted by the English companies, but to which the proposers nevertheless wished to adhere, were printed in an appendix to the published Bible. Publication took place, in the case of the New Testament, on May 17, 1881, and in the case of the canonical books of the Old Testament almost exactly four years later. The revision of the Apocrypha was divided between the two English companies and was taken up by each company on the completion of its main work. The New Testament company distributed Sirach, Tobit, Judith, Wisdom, 1 and 2 Maccabees among three groups of its members, and the Old Testament company appointed a small committee to deal with the remaining books. The work dragged on over many years, involving some inequalities in revision, and ultimately the Apocrypha was published in 1895.

In dealing with the Old Testament the Revisers were not greatly concerned with questions of text. The Massoretic Hebrew text available in 1870 was substantially the same as that which King James' translators had before them, and the criticism of the Septuagint version was not sufficiently advanced to enable them safely to make much use of it except in marginal notes. Their work consisted mainly in the correction of mistranslations that imperfect Hebrew scholarship had left in the Authorized Version. Their changes, as a rule, are slight but tend very markedly to remove obscurities and to improve the intelligibility of the translation. The gain is greatest in the poetical and prophetical books (poetical passages are throughout printed as such, which in itself is a great improvement), and there cannot be much doubt that if the revision of the Old Testament had stood by itself it would have been generally accepted without much opposition. With the new version of the New Testament, the case was different. The changes were necessarily more numerous than in the Old Testament, and the greater familiarity with the New Testament possessed by readers, in general, made the alterations more conspicuous. The New Testament revisers had, in effect, to form a new Greek text before they could proceed to translate it. In this part of their work, they were largely influenced by the presence of Drs. Westcott and Hort, who, as will be shown elsewhere [TEXT OF THE NEW TESTAMENT], were keen and convinced champions of the class of text of which the best representative is the Codex Vaticanus. At the same time Dr. Scrivener, who took a less advanced view of the necessity of changes in the Received Text, was also a prominent member of the company, and it is probably true that not many new readings were adopted which had not the support of Tischendorf and Tregelles, and which would not be regarded by nearly all scholars acquainted with textual criticism as preferable to those of the Authorized Version. To Westcott and Hort may be assigned a large part of the credit for leading the Revisers definitely along the path of critical science; but the Revisers did not follow their leaders the whole way, and their text (edited by Archdeacon Palmer for the Oxford Press in 1881) represents a more conservative attitude than that of the two Cambridge scholars. Nevertheless the amount of textual change was considerable, and to this was added a very large amount of verbal change, sometimes (especially in the Epistles) to secure greater intelligibility, but oftener (and this is more noticeable in the Gospels) to secure uniformity in the translation of Greek words which the Authorized Version deliberately rendered differently in different places (even in parallel narratives of the same event), and precision in the representation of moods and tenses. It was to the great number of changes of this kind, which by themselves appeared needless and pedantic, that most of the criticism bestowed upon the Revised Version was due; but it must be remembered that where the words and phrases of a book are often strained to the uttermost in popular application, it is of great importance that those words and phrases should be as accurately rendered as possible. On the whole, it is certain that the Revised Version marks a great advance on the Authorized Version in respect of accuracy, and the main criticisms to which it is justly open are that the principles of classical Greek were applied too rigidly to Greek which is not classical and that the Revisers, in their careful attention to the Greek, were less happily inspired than their predecessors with the genius of the English language. These defects have no doubt militated against the general acceptance of the Revised Version; but whether they continue to do so or not (and it is to be remembered that we have not yet passed through nearly so long a period as that during which the Authorized Version competed with the Geneva Bible or Jerome's Vulgate with the Old Latin), it is certain that no student of the Bible can afford to neglect the assistance given by the Revised Version towards the true understanding of the Scriptures. In so using it, it should be remembered that renderings which appear in the margin not infrequently represent the views of more than half the Revisers, though they failed to obtain the necessary two-thirds majority. This is perhaps especially the case in the Old Testament, where the Revised Version shows a greater adherence to the Authorized Version than in the New Testament.

It only remains to add that, after the lapse of the 14 years during which it was agreed that no separate American edition should be brought out, while the American appendix continued to appear in the English Revised Version, the American Revisers issued a fresh recension (New Testament in 1900, Old Testament in 1901, without the Apocrypha), embodying not only the readings which appeared in their appendix to the English Revised Version, but also others on which they had since agreed. It is unfortunate that the action originally taken by the English revisers with a view to securing that the two English-speaking nations should continue to have a common Bible should have brought about the opposite result; and though the alterations introduced by the American revisers eminently deserve consideration on their merits, it may be doubted whether the net result is important enough to justify the existence of a separate version. What influence it may have upon the history of the English Bible in the future it is for the future to decide.

CHAPTER 22 The American Standard Version (1901)

The Revised Version, Standard American Edition of the Bible, more commonly known as the American Standard Version (ASV), is a Bible translation into English that was completed in 1901, with the publication of the revision of the Old Testament; the revised New Testament had been released in 1900. It was originally best known by its full name, but soon came to have other names, such as the American Revised Version, the American Standard Revision, the American Standard Revised Bible, and the American Standard Edition. By the time its copyright was renewed in 1929, it had come to be known by its present name, the American Standard Version. Because of its prominence in seminaries, it was sometimes simply called the "Standard Bible" in the United States.

History

The American Standard Version, which was also known as The American Revision of 1901, is rooted in the work begun in 1870 to revise the Authorized Version/King James Bible of 1611. This revision project eventually produced the Revised Version (RV). An invitation was extended to American religious leaders for scholars to work on the RV project. In 1871, thirty scholars were chosen by Philip Schaff. The denominations represented on the American committee were the Baptist, Congregationalist, Dutch Reformed, Friends, Methodist, Episcopal, Presbyterian, Protestant Episcopal, and Unitarian. These scholars began work in 1872. Three of the editors, the youngest in years, became the editors of the American Standard Revised New Testament: Drs. Dwight, Thayer and Matthew Riddle.[80]

Any suggestion of the American Revision Committee would only be accepted if two-thirds of the British Revisers agreed. This principle was

---

[80] Roland H. Worth *Bible Translations: A History Through Source Documents* 1992 p107 "In between these two periods, the American translators continued to meet on a yearly basis to lay plans for the eventual publication of their work. Matthew B. Riddle, the last survivor of the original group of Americans, writes of how the group went about their work: Three of these, the youngest in years, became the editors of the American Standard Revised New Testament: Drs. Dwight, Thayer and Riddle. Dr. Thayer lived to see the published volume, but died a few months afterward ..."

Matthew Brown Riddle, The Story of the Revised New Testament, American Standard Edition (Philadelphia: Sunday School Times, 1908) "Dr. Ezra Abbot was the foremost textual critic in America, and his opinions usually prevailed when questions of text were debated."

backed up by an agreement that if their suggestions were put into the appendix of the RV, the American Committee would not publish their version for 15 years. The appendix had about three hundred suggestions in it.

The Revised Version New Testament was published in 1881, the Old Testament in 1885, and the Apocrypha in 1894. Around this time, the British team disbanded. Also, around this time, unauthorized copied editions of the RV appeared with the suggestions of the American team in the main text. This was possible because while the RV in the UK was the subject of a Crown copyright as a product of the University Presses of Oxford and Cambridge, this protection did not extend to the U.S. and the text was never separately copyrighted there. In 1898, publishers for Oxford and Cambridge Universities published their own editions of the RV with the American suggestions included. However, these suggestions were reduced in number (but it did incorporate all of those suggestions which were listed in the Appendixes, as can be verified by comparing the Appendixes with the main text of the 1898 edition). Some of those Americanized editions by Oxford and Cambridge Universities had the title of "American Revised Version" on the cover of their spines. Some of Thomas Nelson's editions of the American Standard Version Holy Bible included the Apocrypha of the Revised Version. The Revised Version of 1885 and the American Standard Version of 1901 are among the Bible versions authorized to be used in services of the Episcopal Church and the Church of England.[81]

In 1901, after the 15-year deferral agreement between the American and British Revisers expired, and the Revised Version, Standard American Edition, as the ASV Bible was officially called at the time, was published by Thomas Nelson & Sons. It was copyrighted in North America to ensure the

---

[81] The Episcopal Church - American Standard Version of the Bible (1901) - On July 7, 1870, the Convocation of the Province of Canterbury, England, voted to invite some "American divines" to join in the work of revising the Bible. An American Revision Committee was organized on Dec. 7, 1871 and began work on Oct. 4, 1872. In 1901 their work was published as The Holy Bible Containing the Old and New Testaments Translated Out of the Original Tongues, Being the Version Set Forth A.D. 1611 Compared with the Most Ancient Authorities and Revised A.D. 1881-1885. Newly Edited by the American Revision Committee A.D. 1901. Standard Edition. This is one of the versions of the Bible authorized by the Episcopal Church and the Anglican Communion for use in worship.

Versions of Scripture: The Church of England - A Note by the House of Bishops - While the Church of England authorises the Lectionary - what passages are to be read on which occasion - it does not authorize particular translations of the Bible. Nevertheless, among the criteria by which versions of Scripture are judged suitable for reading in church during the course of public worship are the following: 3 Versions of Scripture which are translations and appear to satisfy at least four of the criteria set out in paragraph 1 above include: The Authorized Version or King James Bible (AV), published in 1611, of which a Revised Version was published in 1881-5. Retrieved 5 June 2015.

purity of the ASV text. In 1928, the International Council of Religious Education (the body that later merged with the Federal Council of Churches to form the National Council of Churches) acquired the copyright from Nelson and renewed it the following year. The copyright was a reaction to tampering with the text of the Revised Version by some U.S. publishers, as noted above. By the time the ASV's copyright expired for the final time in 1957,[82] interest in this translation had largely waned in the light of newer and more recent ones, and textual corruption hence never became the issue with the ASV that it had with the RV.

Because the language of the ASV intentionally retained the King James Version's Elizabethan English, was printed with comparatively lower quality materials, and because of what some perceived to be its excessive literalism, it never achieved wide popularity, and the King James Version would remain the primary translation for most American Protestant Christians until the publication of the Revised Standard Version in 1952.

Rationale

There were two rationales for the ASV. One reason was to obviate any justification for the unauthorized copied editions of the RV that had been circulating. Another reason was to use more of the suggestions the American team had preferred, since the British team used few of their suggestions in the first place, even in the later version which they had published incorporating some of them.[citation needed] While many of the suggestions of the American scholars were based on the differences between American and British usage, many others were based on differences in scholarship and what the American revisers felt the best translation to be. Consequently, there were several changes to the KJV text in the ASV that were not present in the RV.

Features

The divine name of the Almighty (the Tetragrammaton) is consistently rendered Jehovah in 6,823 places of the ASV Old Testament, rather than LORD as it appears mostly in the King James Bible and Revised Version of 1881-85. However, there are notably seven verses in the King James Bible where the divine name actually appears which are Genesis 22:14, Exodus 6:3, Exodus 17:15, Judges 6:24, Psalms 83:18, Isaiah 12:2 and Isaiah 26:4 plus as its abbreviated form, Jah, once in Psalms 68:4. The English Revised

---

[82] Bell, Tom. "Trend of Maximum U.S. General Copyright Term". tomwbell.com. Retrieved Tuesday, October 22, 2019.

Version (1881-1885, published with the Apocrypha in 1894) renders the Tetragrammaton as Jehovah where it appears in the King James Version, and another eight times in Exodus 6:2,6–8, Psalm 68:20, Isaiah 49:14, Jeremiah 16:21 and Habakkuk 3:19 plus as its abbreviated form, Jah, twice in Psalms 68:4 and Psalms 89:8. The reason for this change, as the Committee explained in the preface, was that "...the American Revisers... were brought to the unanimous conviction that a Jewish superstition, which regarded the Divine Name as too sacred to be uttered, ought no longer to dominate in the English or any other version of the Old Testament..."[83] Other changes from the RV to the ASV included (but were not limited to) substituting "who" and "that" for "which" when referring to people, and Holy Ghost was dropped in favor of Holy Spirit. Page headings were added and footnotes were improved.

Revisions

The ASV has been the basis of six revisions and one refreshing. They were the Revised Standard Version, 1971 [1946–52] The Revised Standard Version includes two New Testament translation efforts: the 1946 RSV New Testament published alone, with the entire Bible completed in 1952, and then a "second edition of the RSV New Testament, issued in 1971, twenty-five years after its initial publication" not to be confused with the later "New Revised Standard Version" translation effort),[84] the New Revised Standard Version, 1989, the Amplified Bible, 1965, the New American Standard Bible, 1995 [1963–71], the Recovery Version, 1999, the World English Bible, 2000, and the Refreshed American Standard Version New Testament, 2018.[85] The ASV was also the basis for Kenneth N. Taylor's Bible paraphrase, The Living Bible, 1971.

Usage by Jehovah's Witnesses

The ASV has also been used for many years by Jehovah's Witnesses. The reasons for their choosing of the ASV were twofold: its usage of "Jehovah" as the Divine Name, which was a translation of the Tetragrammaton (JHVH) into English as some early Bible scholars had done

---

[83] "Preface", ASV (American ed.), Christian Classics Ethereal Library. It is speculated that because of this, the Jehovah Witness name-dogma was created by Joseph Franklin Rutherford around this time.

[84] New Oxford Annotated Bible - Third Edition "To The Reader" pages xvii & xviii; 2001 Oxford University Press

[85] Refreshed American Standard Version (RASV)

before (i.e. Tyndale at Ps. 83:18).[86] They also derived their name from Isaiah 43:10, 12, both of which contain the phrase, "Ye are my witnesses, saith Jehovah." Also, there was a perception that the ASV had improved the translation of some verses in the King James Version, and in other places it reduced the verses that they found to be erroneously translated in the KJV to mere footnotes, removed from the main text altogether.[87]

The Jehovah's Witnesses' publishing organization, the Watch Tower Bible and Tract Society of Pennsylvania, had printed its own edition of the King James Version since 1926, but did not obtain the rights to print ASV until 1944. From 1944 to 1992, they printed and distributed over a million copies of the ASV. By the 1960s, the New World Translation of the Holy Scriptures, made by members of their group and the rights to which they controlled, had largely replaced ASV as the Bible used most by Witnesses.[88] Though now preferring the NWT, Jehovah's Witnesses' publications frequently quote from other translations, including ASV.[89]

---

[86] "The Tetragrammaton and the Divine Name in the Hebrew Scriptures - NWT". *JW.ORG.*

[87] *"Why a new translation was commissioned", New World Translation of the Holy Scriptures.*

[88] *"Printing and Distributing God's Own Sacred Word", Jehovah's Witnesses – Proclaimers of God's Kingdom, Watch Tower, 1993, p. 607.*

[89] Chapter is by Wikipedia.

CHAPTER 23 The Updated American Standard Version (UASV)

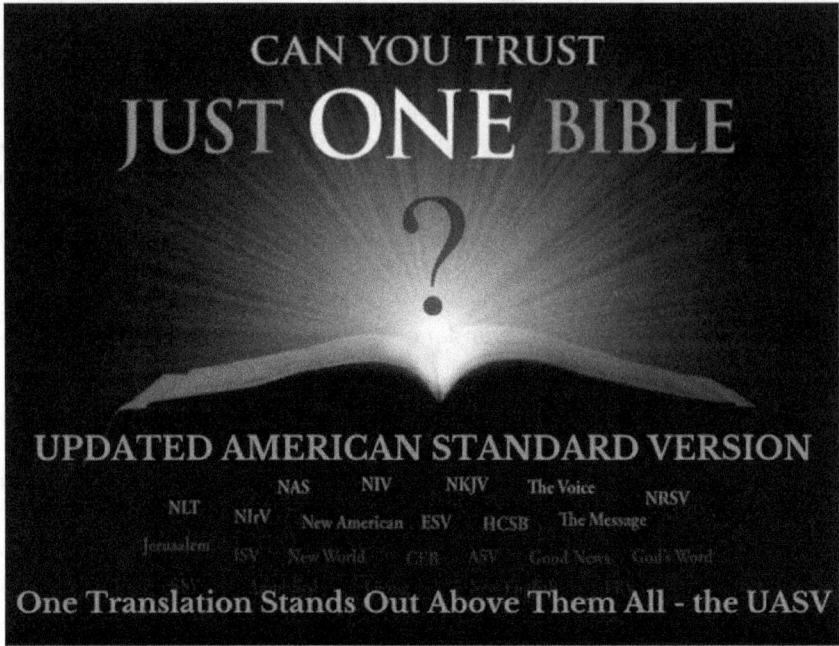

CAN YOU TRUST
JUST ONE BIBLE
?
UPDATED AMERICAN STANDARD VERSION

NAS   NIV   NKJV   The Voice
NLT   NRSV
    NIrV   New American   ESV   HCSB   The Message
Jerusalem   ISV   New World   CEB   ASV   Good News   God's Word
One Translation Stands Out Above Them All - the UASV

Why UASV?

The translation of God's Word from the original languages of Hebrew, Aramaic, and Greek is a task unlike any other and should never be taken lightly. It carries with it the heaviest responsibility: the translator renders God's thoughts into a modern language. The Updated American Standard Version (UASV) is a literal translation. What does that mean?

It means that our primary purpose is to give the Bible readers what God said by way of his human authors, not what a translator thinks God meant in its place.

In other words, our primary goal is to be accurate and faithful to the original text. The meaning of a word is the responsibility of the interpreter (i.e., reader), not the translator.

Updated American Standard Version's Story

It has been a journey filled with many trials and tribulations.

An Idea is Born

In 1986, Edward D. Andrews became a Christian. However, he would fall away from the faith because he lost his faith to Bible critics. It would be in 1996 that he would find his way back. One night in the shower, he began to cry, to cry out to the Father. He pleads with the Father to show him the truth, to help him find the truth. The entire night was spent in prayer and tears. He had made a commitment that if God helped him get the books, he would study and study he did. He studied 6-8 hours a day, seven days a week for ten years. Not wanting to make the mistake that he did before, he studied apologetics, textual criticism, Bible translation process and philosophy, Hebrew, Greek, and many other subject matters, to the tune of over 3,000 books. He had become an apologist for the Bible, the faith and God himself.

In 2005, he decided to become an author. After being rejected by the big publishing houses, he decided to start his own. It was in 2005 that Christian Publishing House was in his mind. Shortly after that, he began publishing other books by Bible scholars. In 2007 he decided to get the official degrees that went with his self-taught education.

EDWARD D. ANDREWS (AS in Criminal Justice, BS in Religion, MA in Biblical Studies, and MDiv in Theology) is CEO and President of Christian Publishing House. He has authored 120 books, including THE TEXT OF THE NEW TESTAMENT, THE COMPLETE GUIDE TO BIBLE TRANSLATION and REASONABLE FAITH. Andrews is the Chief Translator of the Updated American Standard Version (UASV).

Edward D. Andrews is the founder of Christian Publishing House and the Updated American Standard Version. His vision began in 1996.

Trials and Tribulations

In 2008 the economy crashed, and the United States went into a great recession. Andrews had a small business that he was using for his family and funding Christian Publishing House and the Updated American Standard Version when in 2009 many of his clients cut back by removing his services. His business went under, he lost his wife, his house, his truck, and equipment, as well as being forced to move to an apartment. Soon, his finances would not even support the apartment, and he ended up homeless for two years. Through all of this, he continued to pen his books, get his degrees, and maintain his online publishing, as well as publishing other author's books.

He has continued in his fight for the faith, his battle for the Bible, and slowly he is building Christian Publishing House, translating the Updated American Standard Version, and Biblical Training Academy. You can support his translation work here: www.uasvbible.org/donation

OTHER BOOKS BY EDWARD D. ANDREWS

978-1-949586-92-3

978-1-945757-99-0

978-1-949586-91-6

978-0692728710

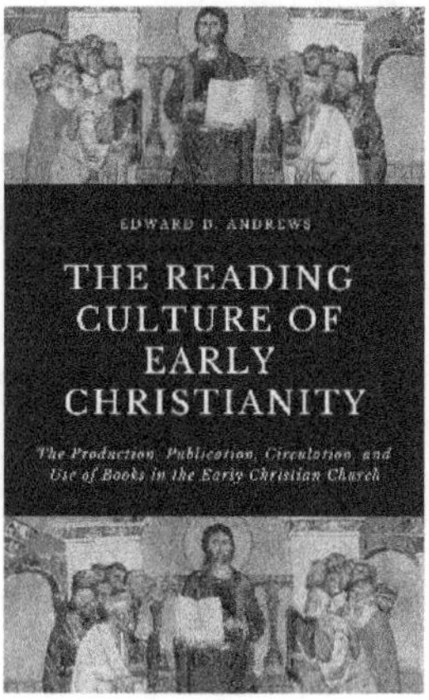

978-1-949586-84-8

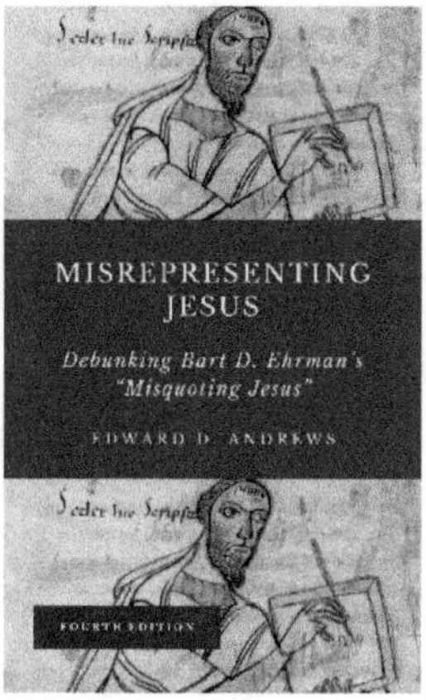

978-1-949586-95-4

THE TEXT OF
THE NEW
TESTAMENT

The Science and Art of Textual Criticism

Don Wilkins
Edward D. Andrews

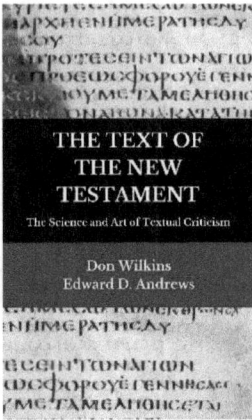

978-1-945757-44-0

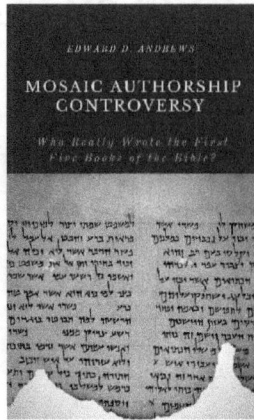

EDWARD D. ANDREWS

MOSAIC AUTHORSHIP
CONTROVERSY

Who Really Wrote the First
Five Books of the Bible?

978-1-949586-79-4

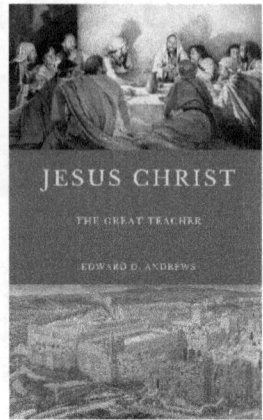

JESUS CHRIST

THE GREAT TEACHER

EDWARD D. ANDREWS

978-1-949586-83-1

Bibliography

Aland, Kurt and Barbara. 1987. *The Text of the New Testament.* Grand Rapids: Eerdmans.

Aland, Kurt, and Barbara Aland. 1995. *The Text of the New Testament.* Grand Rapids: Eerdmans.

Archer, Gleason L. 1994. *A Survey of Old Testament Introduction.* Chicago: Moody.

—. 1982. *Encyclopedia of Bible Difficulties.* Grand Rapids: Zondervan.

Arduini, Stefano, and Robert Hodgson Jr. 2004. *Similarities and Differences in Translation.* New York: American Bible Society.

Arndt, William, Frederick W. Danker, and Walter Bauer. 2000. *A Greek-English Lexicon of the New Testament and Other Early Christian Literature. 3rd ed.* . Chicago: University of Chicago Press.

Baer, Daniel. 2007. *The Unquenchable Fire.* Maitland, FL: Xulon Press.

Barnett, Paul. 2005. *The Birth of Christianity: The First Twenty Years (After Jesus, Vol. 1)* . Grand Rapids, MI: Wm. B. Eerdmans .

Barnwell, Katharine. 1975. *Bible Translation: An Introductory Course in Translation Principles.* Kenya: SIL International.

—. 1974. *Introduction to Semantics and Translation.* England: SIL.

Beekman, John, and John Callow. 1974. *Translating the Word of God.* Grand Rapids: Zondervan.

Bercot, David W. 1998. *A Dictionary of Early Christian Beliefs.* Peabody: Hendrickson.

Bock, Darrell L. 2006. *The Missing Gospels: Unerthing the Truth Behind Alternative Christianities.* Nashville, TN: Thomas Nelson.

Bock, Darrell L, and Daniel B Wallace. 2007. *Dethroning Jesus: Exposing Popular Culture's Quest to Unseat the Biblical Christ.* Nashville: Thomas Nelson.

Borgen, Peder. 1997. *Philo of Alexandria: An Exegete for His Time.* Leiden, Boston: Brill.

Brand, Chad, Charles Draper, and England Archie. 2003. *Holman Illustrated Bible Dictionary: Revised, Updated and Expanded.* Nashville, TN: Holman.

Bray, Gerald. 2010. *Translating the Bible: From William Tyndale to King James.* London: The Latimer Trust.

Bruce, F. F. 1981. *The New Testament Documents: Are they Reliable?* Downer Groves: Inter Varsity. Accessed April 03, 2009. http://www.libertyparkusafd.org/lp/Burgon/cd-roms/121bible.html.

Bruce, F. F., J. I. Packer, Philip Cmfort, and Carl F. H. Henry. 1992, 2003. *The Origin of the Bible.* Carol Steam, IL: Tyndale House.

Campbell, Gordon. 2010. *The Holy Bible: King James Version, Quatercentenary Edition.* Oxford, England, UK: Oxford University Press.

Comfort, Philip. 2005. *Encountering the Manuscripts: An Introduction to New Testament Paleography and Textual Criticism.* Nashville: Broadman & Holman.

—. 2005. *Encounterring the Manuscripts: An Introduction to New Testament Paleography and Textual Criticism.* Nashville: Broadman & Holman.

Comfort, Philip W. 2000. *Essential Guide to Bible Versions.* Wheaton: Tyndale House.

Comfort, Philip W. 2008. *New Testament Text and Translation Commentary.* Carol Stream: Tyndale House Publishers.

Comfort, Philip Wesley. 1992. *The Quest for the Original Text of the New Testament.* Eugene: Wipf and Stock.

Comfort, Philip, and David Barret. 2001. *The Text of the Earliest New Testament Greek Manuscripts.* Wheaton: Tyndale House Publishers.

Cruse, C. F. 1998. *Eusebius' Eccliatical History.* Peabody, MA: Hendrickson.

Dever, William G. 2001. *What Did the Biblical Writers Know, and When Did They Know It?* Grand Rapids: William B. Eerdmans Publishing Company.

Dewey, David. 2004. *A User's Guide to Bible Translation: Making the Most of Different Versions.* Downers Grove : InterVaristy Press.

Durant, Will & Ariel. 1950. *The Story of Civilization: Part IV—The Age of Faith.* New York, NY: Simon & Schuster.

Edwards, Tyron. 1908. *A Dictionary of Thoughts.* Detroit: F. B. Dickerson Company.

Ehrman, Bart D. 2005. *Misquoting Jesus: The Story Behind Who Changed the Bible and Why.* New York: Harper One.

Ehrman, Bart D. Holmes, Michael W. 1995. *The Text of the New Testament in Contemporary Research: Essays on the Status Quaestionis .* Grand Rapids, MI: Eerdmans.

Ehrman, Bart D. 2003. *Lost Christianities: The Battles for Scripture and the Faiths We Never Knew .* New York: Oxford University Press.

Elwell, Walter A. 2001. *Evangelical Dictionary of Theology (Second Edition).* Grand Rapids: Baker Academic.

Elwell, Walter A, and Philip Wesley Comfort. 2001. *Tyndale Bible Dictionary.* Wheaton, Ill: Tyndale House Publishers.

Evans, Craig A. 2002. *Fabricating Jesus: How Modern Scholars Distort the Gospels.* Downers Grove, IL: InterVaristy Press.

F. Garcia Martinez, Julio Barrera, Trebolle, Florentino Garcia Martinez, and J. Trebolle Barrera. 1995. *The People of the Dead Sea Scrolls: Their Writings, Beliefs and Practices.* Leiden: Brill Academic.

Ferguson, Everett. 2003. *Backgrounds of Early Christianity.* Grand Rapids, MI: Wm. B. Eerdmans.

Gamble, Henry Y. 1995. *Books and Readers in the Early Church: A History of Early Christian Texts.* New Haven: New Haven University Press.

Geisler, Norman L. 2007. *A Popular Survey of the New Testament.* Grand Rapids: Baker Books.

—. 2012. *Defending Inerrancy: Affirming the Accuracy of Scripture for a New Generation.* Grand Rapids, MI: Baker Books.

—. 1980. *Inerrancy.* Grand Rapids, MI: Zondervan.

Geisler, Norman L, and William E Nix. 1996. *A General Introduction to the Bible.* Chicago: Moody Press.

Geisler, Norman L. 1981. *Biblical Errancy: An Analysis of Its Philosophical Roots.* Eugene, OR: Wipf and Stock Publisher.

Geisler, Norman L., and Thomas Howe. 1992. *The Big Book of Bible Difficulties.* Grand Rapids: Baker Books.

Green, Joel B, Scot McKnight, and Howard Marshall. 1992. *Dictionary of Jesus and the Gospels.* Downers Grove, IL: InterVarsity Press.

Greenlee, J Harold. 1995. *Introduction to New Testament Textual Criticism.* Peabody: Hendrickson.

Greenslade, S. L. 1975. *The Cambridge History of the Bible, Vol. 3: The West from the Reformation to the Present Day.* Cambridge University Press: Cambridge.

Grudem, Wayne, Leland Ryken, John C Collins, Vern S Poythress, and Bruce Winter. 2005. *Translating Truth: The Case for Essentially Literal Bible Translation.* Wheaton: Crossway Books.

Hendriksen, William, and Simon J. Kistemaker. 1953–2001. *Exposition of I-II Thessalonians, vol. 3, New Testament Commentary.* Grand Rapids: Baker Book House.

Hill, Charles E., and Michael J. Kruger. 2012. *The Early Text of the New Testament.* Oxford: Oxford University Press.

Hoffman, Joel M. 2007. *AND GOD SAID: How Translations Conceal the Bible's Original Meaning.* New York, NY: Thomas Dunne Books.

Holmes, Michael W. 2007. *The Apostolic Fathers: Greek Texts and English Translations.* Grand Rapids: Baker Academics.

Hurtado, Larry W. 2006. *The Earliest Christian Artifacts: Manuscripts and Christian Origins.* Grand Rapids: Eerdmans.

James, M R. 1924, 2004. *The Apocryphal New Testament.* Berkeley, CA: Apocryphile Press.

Johnson, William A, and Holt N Parker. 2011. *Ancient Literacies: The Culture of Reading in Greece and Rome.* Oxford: Oxford University Press.

Jones, Timothy Paul. 2007. *Misquoting Truth: A Guide to the Fallacies of Bart Ehrman's Misquoting Jesus.* Downer Groves: InterVarsity Press.

Kaiser, Walter C, Peter H Davids, and Frederick Fyvie , Brauch, Manfred T Bruce. 1996. *Hard Sayings of the Bible.* Downer Groves, IL: Inter Varsity Press.

Keener, Craig S. 1993. *The IVP Bible Background Commentary: New Testament.* Downer Groves, IL: InterVarsity Press.

Kenyon, F. G. 2006. *The Palaeography of Greek Papyri.* Whitefish: Kessinger Publishing.

Kistemaker, Simon J, and William Hendriksen. 1953-2001. *New Testament Commentary: Exposition of the Acts of the Apostles* . Grand Rapids, MI: Baker Book House.

Komoszewski, J. Ed, James M. Sawyer, and Daniel Wallace. 2006. *Reinventing Jesus* . Grand Rapids, MI: Kregel Publications.

Lightfoot, Neil R. 1963, 1988, 2003. *How We Got the Bible.* Grand Rapids, MI: Baker Books.

Lindsell, Harold. 1976. *The Battle for the Bible.* Grand Rapids: Zondervan.

Linnemann. 1992. *Is There A Synoptic Problem? Rethinking the Literary Dependance of the First Three Gospels.* Grand Rapids, MI: Baker Book House.

Linnemann, Eta. 2001. *Biblical Criticism on Trial: How Scientific is "Scientific Theology"?* Grand Rapids: Kregel.

McDonald, Lee Martin. July 13, 2009. *Forgotten Scriptures: The Selection and Rejection of Early Religious Writings.* Louisville: Westminster John Knox Press .

Metzger, Bruce M. 1964, 1968, 1992. *The Text of the New Testament: Its Transmission, Corruption, and Transmission.* New York: Oxford University Press.

Metzger, Bruce M. 1994. *A Textual Commentary on the Greek New Testament.* New York: United Bible Society.

Metzger, Bruce M., and Bart D. Ehrman. 2005. *The Text of the New Testament: Its Transmission, Corruption, and Restoration (4th Edition).* New York: Oxford University Press.

—. 1964, 1968, 1992, 205. *The Text of the New Testament: Its Transmission, Corruption, and Transmission.* New York: Oxford University Press.

Metzger, Bruce. 2001. *The Bible in Translation: Ancient and English Versions.* Grand Rapids: Baker Academic.

Milligan, George. 2009. *The New Testament Documents, Their Origin and Early History* . New York, NY: General Books LLC.

Mounce, William D. 2006. *Mounce's Complete Expository Dictionary of Old & New Testament Words.* Grand Rapids, MI: Zondervan.

Munday, Jeremy. 2009. *Introducing Translation Studies: Theories and Applications (2bd Edition).* London: Routledge.

Oates, John F., Alan E. Samuel, and Bradford C. Welles. 1967. *Yale Papyri in the Beinecke Rare Book and Manuscript Library* . (New Haven: American Society of Papyrologists.

Orchard, Bernard. 1776-1976, 2005. *J. J. Griesbach: Synoptic and Text - Critical Studies* . Cambridge: Cambridge University Press.

Packer, J. I. 1965. *God Speaks to Man: Revelation and the Bible.* Atlanta: Westminster Press.

Pagels, Elaine. 1989. *The Gnostic Gospels.* New York: Vintage.

Parker, David C. 1997. *The living Text of the Gospels.* Cambridge: Cambridge University Press.

Porter, Stanley E, and Mark J Boda. 2009. *Translating the New Testament.* Grand Rapids, MI: Wm. B. Eerdmans.

Porter, Stanley E, and Richard S Hess. 2004. *Translating the Bible: Problems and Prospects.* New York, NY: T&T Clark International.

Poythress, Vern S. Grudem, Wayne A. 2004. *The TNIV and The Gender-Neutral Bible Controversy.* Nashville: Boardman & Holman.

Price, Randall. 2007. *Searching for the Original Bible.* Eugene: Harvest House.

Ray, Vernon. 1982. "The Formal vs Dynamic Equivalent Principle in New Testament Translation." *Restoration Quarterly 25* 46-56.

Rhodes, Ron. 2009. *The Complete Guid to Bible Translations.* Eugene, OR: Harvest House.

Richards, E. Randolph. 2004. *Paul And First-Century Letter Writing: Secretaries, Composition and Collection.* Downers Grove: InterVarsity Press.

Roberts, Alexander, and James Donaldson. 1994. *The Ante-Nicene Fathers.* Peabody: Hendrickson.

Roberts, C. H. 1970. *Books in the Graeco-Roman World and in the New Testament in the Cambridge History of the Bible, Vol. 1, From the Beginnings to Jerome* . Cambridge: Cambridge University Press.

Roberts, Colin H. 1979. *Manuscript, Society, and Belief in Early Christian Egypt*. London: Oxford University Press.

Roberts, Colin H., and Theodore C. Skeat. 1987. *The Birth of the Codex*. London: Oxford University Press.

Robertson, A. T. 1925. *An Introduction to the Textual Criticism of the New Testament*. London: Hodder & Stoughton.

Royse, James R. 2008. *Scribal Habits in Early Greek New Testament Papyri (New Testament Tools and Studies) (New Testament Tools, Studies and Documents)*. Leiden & Boston: Brill Academic Pub.

Ryken, Leland. 2005. *Choosing a Bible: Understanding Bible Translation Differences*. Wheaton: Crossway Books.

—. 2002. *The Word of God in English*. Wheaton: Crossway Books.

—. 2009. *Understanding English Bible Translation: The Case for an Essentially Literal Approach*. Wheaton, IL: Crossway Books.

Schurer, Emil. 1890. *A HISTORY OF THE JEWISH PEOPLE IN THE TIME OF JESUS CHRIST (Volume II)*. Edinburgh: T. & T. Clark.

Scorgie, Glen G, Mark L Strauss, and Stephen M Voth. 2003. *The Challenge of Bible Translation*. Grand Rapids: Zondervan.

Scott, Julius J. Jr. 1995. *Jewish Backgrounds of the New Testament*. Grand Rapids, MI: Baker Academic.

Souter, Alexander. 1913. *The Text and Canon of the New Testament*. New York: Charles Scribner's Sons.

Thomas, Robert L. 2000. *How to Choose a Bible Version*. Scotland: Christian Focus Publications.

—. 2002. *Three Views of the Origins of the Synoptic Gospels*. Grand Rapids, MI: Kregel.

Thomas, Robert L., and F. David Farnell. 1998. *THE JESUS CRISIS: The Inroads of Historical Criticism in Evagelical Scholarship*. Grand Rapids, MI: Kregel Publications.

Thompson, Edward Maunde. 1896. *Bible Illustrations*. Oxford; London:: Oxford University Press.

Torrey, Reuben Archer. 1907. *Difficulties in the Bible: Alleged Errors and Contradictions*. Chicago: Moody Press.

University, Stanford. 2012. *Calculating the Time and Cost of Paul's Missionary Journeys.* Accessed 07 12, 2014. http://www.openbible.info/blog/2012/07/calculating-the-time-and-cost-of-pauls-missionary-journeys/.

Vine, W E. 1996. *Vine's Expository Dictionary of Old and New Testament Words.* Nashville: Thomas Nelson.

Virkler, Henry A, and Karelynne Gerber Ayayo. 1981, 2007. *Hermeneutics: Principles and Processes of Biblical Interpretation.* Grand Rapids, MI: Baker Academic.

Wallace, Daniel B. 2008. *bible.org.* Winter. Accessed December 18, 2011. http://bible.org/article/number-textual-variants-evangelical-miscalculation.

—. 2011. *Revisiting the Corruption of the New Testament: Manuscript, Patristic, and Apocryphal Evidence.* Grand Rapids, MI: Kregel Publications.

Wallace, Daniel. 2011. *The Reliability of the New Testament: Bart Ehrman and Daniel Wallace in Dialogue.* Minneapolis, MN: Fortress Press.

Wallace, Robert Burns. 1929. *An Introduction to the Bible as Literature.* London, England, UK: Westminster Press.

Walton, John H., Victor H. Matthews, and Mark W Chavalas. 2000. *The IVP Bible Background Commentary: Old Testament.* Downers Grove: IVP Academic.

Wegner, Paul D. 2006. *A Student's Guide to Textual Criticism of the Bible: Its History Methods & Results.* Downers Grove: InterVarsity Press.

Westcott, B. F., and F. J. A. Hort. 1882. *The New Testament in the Original Greek, Vol. 2: Introduction, Appendix.* London: Macmillan and Co.

Westcott, B. F., and Hort F. J. A. 1882. *The New Testament in the Original Greek, Vol. 2: Introduction, Appendix.* London: Macmillan and Co.

Whiston, William. 1987. *The Works of Josephus.* Peabody, MA: Hendrickson.